SUBMARINES

■■■■■■■■■■■■■■■■■■■■■■■■■■■■

Probing the Ocean Depths

These and other books are included in the Encyclopedia of Discovery and Invention series:

Airplanes	Movies
Anesthetics	Phonograph
Animation	Photography
Atoms	Plate Tectonics
Automobiles	Printing Press
Clocks	Radar
Computers	Radios
Genetics	Railroads
Germs	Ships
Gravity	Submarines
Guns	Telephones
Human Origins	Telescopes
Lasers	Television
Microscopes	Vaccines

SUBMARINES
Probing the Ocean Depths

by SEAN M. GRADY

The ENCYCLOPEDIA of
D·I·S·C·O·V·E·R·Y
and **INVENTION**

P.O. Box 289011 SAN DIEGO, CA 92198-9011

Library of Congress Cataloging-in-Publication Data

Grady, Sean M., 1965-
    Submarines : probing the ocean depths / by Sean M. Grady
    p. cm.—(The Encyclopedia of discovery and invention)
    Includes bibliographical references and index.
    Summary: Discusses the development of submarines and
the history of their uses.
    ISBN 1-56006-227-4
    1. Submarine boats—History—Juvenile literature.
    2. Underwater navigation—History—Juvenile literature
    [1. Submarines—History.]   I. Title.   II. Series.
    VM365.G72   1994
    623.8'205—dc20   91-20628
                                                              CIP
                                                              AC

Contents

▪▪▪▪▪▪▪▪▪▪▪▪▪▪▪▪▪▪▪▪▪▪▪▪▪▪▪▪▪▪▪▪▪▪▪▪▪▪

Foreword   7
Introduction   10

CHAPTER 1 ▪ Experiments in Submerged Sailing   12
          Van Drebbel's underwater boat;
          From oddities to submersibles;
          Bushnell's *Turtle*;
          The way is set.

CHAPTER 2 ▪ Submarines from New Jersey   24
          Holland pioneers submarine design;
          The *Fenian Ram* takes to the water;
          The *Plunger*;
          Lake takes the lead.

CHAPTER 3 ▪ Unseen Tools of War   38
          Submarine combat in World War I;
          The first submarine fleets;
          German U-boat action;
          Combat at sea;
          Developments during wartime.

CHAPTER 4 ▪ Wartime Workhorses   49
          Larger, mightier submarines;
          Stockpiling for war;
          From hunters to hunted;
          Menacing tools of war.

CHAPTER 5 ▪ Weapons of Deterrence   61
          The atomic submarine is born;
          Development of the nuclear navy;
          New designs, new duties;
          Missile-carrying subs;
          Submarine warfare in modern times.

CHAPTER 6 ■ The Future   73
        Reductions in military fleets;
        Pleasures of underwater travel;
        Vessels of scientific exploration;
        Deep water research on the NR-1.

Glossary   85
For Further Reading   87
Works Consulted   89
Index   90
About the Author   95
Picture Credits   96

Foreword

The belief in progress has been one of the dominant forces in Western Civilization from the Scientific Revolution of the seventeenth century to the present. Embodied in the idea of progress is the conviction that each generation will be better off than the one that preceded it. Eventually, all peoples will benefit from and share in this better world. R.R. Palmer, in his *History of the Modern World*, calls this belief in progress "a kind of nonreligious faith that the conditions of human life" will continually improve as time goes on.

For over a thousand years prior to the seventeenth century, science had progressed little. Inquiry was largely discouraged, and experimentation, almost nonexistent. As a result, science became regressive and discovery was ignored. Benjamin Farrington, a historian of science, characterized it this way: "Science had failed to become a real force in the life of society. Instead there had arisen a conception of science as a cycle of liberal studies for a privileged minority. Science ceased to be a means of transforming the conditions of life." In short, had this intellectual climate continued, humanity's future would have been little more than a clone of its past.

Fortunately, these circumstances were not destined to last. By the seventeenth and eighteenth centuries, Western society was undergoing radical and favorable changes. And the changes that occurred gave rise to the notion that progress was a real force urging civilization forward. Surpluses of consumer goods were replacing substandard living conditions in most of Western Europe. Rigid class systems were giving way to social mobility. In nations like France and the United States, the lofty principles of democracy and popular sovereignty were being painted in broad, gilded strokes over the fading canvases of monarchy and despotism.

But more significant than these social, economic, and political changes, the new age witnessed a rebirth of science. Centuries of scientific stagnation began crumbling before a spirit of scientific inquiry that spawned undreamed of technological advances. And it was the discoveries and inventions of scores of men and women that fueled these new technologies, dramatically increasing the ability of humankind to control nature—and, many believed, eventually to guide it.

It is a truism of science and technology that the results derived from observation and experimentation are not finalities. They are part of a process. Each discovery is but one piece in a continuum bridging past and present and heralding an extraordinary future. The heroic age of the Scientific Revolution was simply a start. It laid a foundation upon which succeeding generations of imaginative thinkers could build. It kindled the belief that progress is possible as long as there were gifted men and women who would respond to society's needs. When Antonie van Leeuwenhoek observed *Animalcules* (little animals) through his high-powered microscope in 1683, the discovery did not end there. Others followed who would call these "little animals" bacteria and, in time, recognize their role in the process of health and disease. Robert Koch, a German bacteriologist and winner of the Nobel Prize in Physiology and Medicine, was one of these men. Koch firmly established that bacteria are responsible for causing infectious diseases. He identified, among others, the causative organisms of anthrax and tuberculosis. Alexander Fleming, another Nobel Laureate, progressed still further in the quest to understand and control bacteria. In 1928, Fleming discovered penicillin, the antibiotic wonder drug. Penicillin, and the generations of antibiotics that succeeded it, have done more to prevent premature death than any other discovery in the history of humankind. And as civilization hastens toward the twenty-first century, most agree that the conquest of van Leeuwenhoek's "little animals" will continue.

The *Encyclopedia of Discovery and Invention* examines those discoveries and inventions that have had a sweeping impact on life and thought in the modern world. Each book explores the ideas that led to the invention or discovery, and, more importantly, how the world changed and continues to change because of it. The series also highlights the people behind the achievements—the unique men and women whose singular genius and rich imagination have altered the lives of everyone. Enhanced by photographs and clearly explained technical drawings, these books are comprehensive examinations of the building blocks of human progress.

SUBMARINES

Probing the Ocean Depths

SUBMARINES

Introduction

On a sunny day in 1621 people living in London saw a strange craft ply its way along the river Thames. The thing looked much like an ordinary fishing boat, except that it had unusually high sides and was covered with a tight skin of leather. Its twelve oars stuck out through leather fittings in the side of the hull. Its crew climbed in through a wood-and-leather cover that could be sealed tightly at the top. And, as the people watched, it suddenly sank, traveled downstream, and came back to the surface like some weird man-made fish.

The boat's inventor, Cornelius van Drebbel, was simply testing an idea. Yet his invention marked the first step in the centuries-long development of the submarine, a vessel that would be able to travel underwater guided by its crew. Over the next 180 years many inventors followed van Drebbel's lead. Many failed, spending years on their projects only to end up with large, complex pieces of junk. Some of this work, however, yielded small successes that inspired other inventors. Finally, two men living in New Jersey in the 1890s hit upon similar designs that allowed sailors to travel beneath the waves.

To most admirals and other high-ranking officers who spent their careers on surface ships, these boats (as submarines traditionally are called) were not devices of honorable warfare. Instead, these officers saw them as the modern equivalent of pirate ships that

... TIMELINE: SUBMARINES

1   2   3   4

1 ■ 1621
Cornelius van Drebbel builds the first of three submersible rowboats.

2 ■ 1776
David Bushnell's *Turtle* carries out the first submarine attack against a surface warship.

3 ■ 1800
Robert Fulton builds the *Nautilus*, a hand-cranked submarine.

4 ■ 1850
Wilhelm Bauer builds the treadmill-driven *Brandtaucher* (*Sea Diver*).

5 ■ 1881
John Holland launches the *Fenian Ram*, the first working submarine powered by a gasoline engine.

6 ■ 1893
Holland wins a U.S. government contract to build the *Plunger*, a steam-driven submarine.

7 ■ 1897
Simon Lake builds the *Argonaut*, a submarine that dives and surfaces with an even horizontal motion.

8 ■ 1900
U.S. Navy commissions the USS *Holland*, its first functional submarine.

9 ■ 1914
Outbreak of World War I; ten German U-boats set out on world's first submarine patrol.

attacked surface ships without warning. Indeed, when Germany began using submarines to sink British and American merchant ships during World War I, military and civilian leaders in other nations criticized the attacks as treacherous and cowardly. Few navies, including those with submarine fleets, thought that subs would ever equal surface warships in combat.

Later developments proved this opinion wrong. The creation of these submersible, or underwater, warships, which could attack without warning from their ocean hiding places, forever changed the way navies, and nations, go to war. In two world wars submarines wreaked havoc on war fleets and merchant shipping. Later, during the cold war between the United States and the Soviet Union, each superpower used submarines to keep the other in check.

With the fall of the Soviet Union and the end of the cold war, scientists and inventors can focus their attention on nonmilitary uses for submarines. Submersible research vessels have already begun to reveal the secrets of the world's oceans. With these vessels scientists have studied the behavior of many undersea plants and animals and have explored some of the mysterious rock formations that make up the ocean floor. New voyages are planned, and these will probably travel far deeper than any have ever gone before. From such voyages new discoveries can lead to future undersea exploration—and new types of submersibles—thus assuring the advancement of submarine technology for years to come.

> 7 > 8 > 9 > 10 > 11 > 12 > 13 > 14 > 15 >

10 ■ 1939
Outbreak of World War II; the German U-30 sinks the British passenger liner *Athenia*.

11 ■ 1954
The USS *Nautilus*, the world's first nuclear-powered submarine, is launched in Groton, Connecticut.

12 ■ 1958
The Soviet Union launches its first nuclear-powered, ballistic missile equipped submarine.

13 ■ 1959
The USS *Skate* breaks through the Arctic ice pack and surfaces at the North Pole.

14 ■ 1985
The first short-range tourist submarines go into business.

15 ■ 1993
A Japanese remote-controlled, robotic submersible is set for descent to the Challenger Deep in preparation for later, crewed submersible dives.

CHAPTER 1

Experiments in Submerged Sailing

The idea of submarine travel, or travel beneath the ocean in a self-contained vessel, has been around for thousands of years. One of the earliest records of anyone attempting to explore the underwater world in such a vessel can be traced to the fourth century B.C. and a legend about Alexander the Great. Alexander ruled the ancient kingdom of Macedonia, a land bordering the Aegean Sea north of modern Greece. From 336 to 323 B.C. he and his armies conquered lands from Greece to Egypt and western India.

According to the legend Alexander once visited the floor of the Mediter-

Legend has it that Alexander the Great made an underwater trip in a glass barrel or a wooden barrel fitted with glass windows.

ranean Sea. The craft he used for this journey is somewhat of a mystery. It has been described by historians both as a wooden barrel fitted with glass windows and as a barrel made entirely of glass. Alexander was sealed inside and lowered underwater from a boat, and hauled back up before the air inside the vessel ran out. The legend does not say whether or not Alexander was the only person to make such an underwater trip. It does say, however, that when he returned to the surface, Alexander told of all sorts of strange beasts and unusual landscapes he had seen through the craft's glass panels.

Other explorers and inventors are said to have experimented with a way to sail beneath the waves. The great artist and inventor Leonardo da Vinci supposedly once developed a device that allowed people to breathe and work underwater. However, he wrote in his diary that he had destroyed these plans "on account of the evil nature of men who [would] practice assassination at the bottom of the sea."

A Submersible Boat

The first known serious attempt to design and build underwater vessels was made in England in the early seventeenth century. The inventor was a Dutch physician, Cornelius van Drebbel, who was living in London as a guest of King James I. One day in 1620 van

Cornelius van Drebbel's inspiration for creating an underwater vessel came from watching the bobbing motions of a fishing boat towing heavy loads.

Drebbel was watching a group of fishing boats row up the Thames River. It was late in the afternoon, and the fishermen were towing the day's catch in baskets behind their boats. As he watched, van Drebbel noticed that the boats dipped and rose in the water with each stroke of their oars. This phenomenon puzzled the doctor.

After studying the boats for a few minutes, van Drebbel realized what was making them dip and rise. The baskets of fish the boats were towing were acting like brakes against the water. As the boats tried to move forward, the baskets pulled backward, forcing the boats lower in the water. Pondering the forces at work among the boats, the baskets, and the river, van Drebbel had an idea. If a group of oarsmen rowed fast while towing a heavy weight, he thought, would they be able to force their boat all the way underwater? Van Drebbel thought this might be possible. And if the boat was covered and watertight, he reasoned, its crew might be able to continue its journey by rowing underwater.

Van Drebbel was intrigued by the possibility of building a submersible, or underwater, boat. He decided to ask his host, King James, for permission and money to build his boat and test it in the Thames. Though van Drebbel was mainly interested in seeing if his idea would work, the king saw the proposed craft as a possible tool of war in the island kingdom's sea battles. James agreed to pay for the materials and workmen that the physician needed for his experiment. For the next few months van Drebbel worked on his plans, building models that towed wood and metal weights. Before long, though, he discovered that his design was flawed. No matter how many oarsmen his boats carried, they could not go fast enough to force the boat underwater. Every time the rowers completed a stroke, the boat bobbed back up.

Van Drebbel soon realized his mistake. The oarsmen would never be able to row hard or fast enough to sink the light boat. What van Drebbel needed was a way of adding weight, or ballast, to the boat so it would sink on its own, along with a method for discarding weight so it could return to the surface. He had a true challenge before him. Simply loading rocks or other weights on the boat would allow it to sink easily enough. And if the weights were carried in a specially rigged sling, the boat's crew could drop them underwater and allow the boat to rise. But van Drebbel wanted his boat to submerge and ascend at will, rather than being stuck on the surface once the weight was gone.

After pondering the problem, van Drebbel hit upon a simple method, one that is essentially the same as that used in modern submarines. Since the boat was going to sail underwater, he reasoned, why not let the water do some of the work? Abandoning his idea of a towed weight, van Drebbel redesigned his boat to use water as a renewable, or reusable, form of ballast. Inside its covered hull the boat carried two rows of bags made of greased pigskins. The necks of these bags were tied to short brass tubes that stuck out through holes in the hull. Wooden handles were lashed to the other ends of the bags. To submerge the boat, the crew let the bags fill with water. To raise the boat the crew twisted the bags with the handles, squeezing out enough water to let the boat float to the surface.

This small design change allowed van Drebbel to create the first working submersible boat in 1621. Of course, there were many drawbacks to the Dutch physician's design. Since the boat used oars to move through the water, the oarsmen had to make sure they turned their oar blades flat on their return strokes. Otherwise, as they pushed the oars back, they would row the boat in the direction it came from, resulting in its staying dead in the water. They also could not row very fast—no more

than walking speed—nor could they row far before they tired or ran out of air.

Even so, the boat was good enough for van Drebbel's purposes, and he used it and two larger boats he later built to make a number of voyages along the Thames. King James himself reportedly took an underwater trip in one of van Drebbel's boats, traveling up and down the river for a couple of hours.

How van Drebbel was able to keep the air fresh for so long is unknown. Some scholars suggest that he built his boats with a pair of air pipes connected to a hand-operated bellows. This method could be used to draw fresh air in from one pipe and expel stale air from the second. Other historians, how-

King James I financed van Drebbel's work on a submersible boat. He hoped to use the boats to achieve victories at sea.

ever, suggest that van Drebbel had either discovered a way to separate pure oxygen out of the air and carry it in special tanks or developed a method of absorbing carbon dioxide from the air in the boat. Many of these scholars think that the latter method is probably the one he used.

Despite its success van Drebbel's little submarine never developed into more than a novelty. For one thing, its uses were limited by its small size (the largest could hold only twelve oarsmen and a handful of passengers) and slow speed. For another, King James, van Drebbel's patron, died in 1625, five years into the project. Nevertheless, van Drebbel continued working on his design for the British Admiralty until he died in 1634. Nothing is known about any improvements he made in his boat's design. King James's son and successor, Charles I, ordered that the inventor's later work be made a national secret, to be revealed only to the kings and queens of England. Despite this proclamation of secrecy, van Drebbel's early work proved that underwater travel, however limited, was possible.

From Oddities to Operational Submersibles

Few inventors tackled the challenge of making a workable submarine in the next hundred years or so. Those who did met with little success. But this did not prevent some of them from making grand claims about their inventions.

A French-born inventor known only as De Son was among those who bragged of his accomplishments in this area. In 1653 De Son trumpeted his invention—a clockwork-driven boat—as the wonder-ship of the seventeenth century. The inventor declared that his submarine, which had rams fore and aft (front and back) for punching holes in ships' hulls, would be able to destroy one hundred ships in a day without risk of being touched by "fire, nor storm, or bullets . . . unless it please God." Furthermore, De Son said, the clockwork engine would drive the sub underwater from Rotterdam, the Netherlands, to London and back, a journey of more than four hundred miles, in one day. Despite his grand declarations, De Son never managed to get the submarine to work. He eventually turned it into a public attraction, charging people to look at his "Strange Ship," as he called it.

The world had to wait until the American Revolution before it heard of another successful underwater boat. In 1775 a Connecticut farmer named David Bushnell began building a secret weapon he hoped could be used against the British Royal Navy in the coming war between Great Britain and its American colonies.

Although there are no records of where Bushnell got the idea for his submarine, it is obvious how the vessel got its name: the *Turtle*. Seen from the front, the *Turtle* resembled two large turtle shells pasted together and standing on end. The vessel actually was built from long strips of wood mounted on large iron hoops. Seen from the side, the turtle shell shape was even more pronounced. A short viewing port made of brass, iron, and glass on top of the craft looked somewhat like a turtle's head poking halfway out. The top of this structure—a forerunner of the conning towers that house the control centers on twentieth-century submarines—also formed the *Turtle*'s hatch. A pair of

BUSHNELL'S *TURTLE*

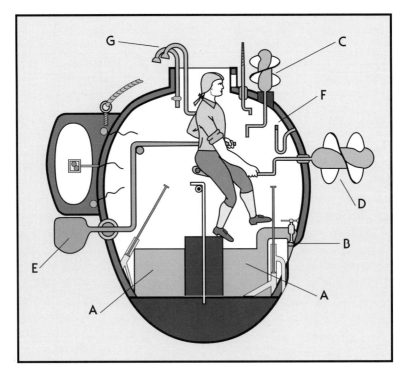

When David Bushnell designed the *Turtle* in 1776, he offered ingenious solutions to the four major problems faced by designers of submersible craft: submergence, propulsion, navigation, and air supply.

To submerge the one-person craft, Bushnell placed ballast tanks (A) at the bottom of the *Turtle*. The tanks were equipped with a flooding valve (B) that allowed sea water to rush into the tanks. The weight of the water brought the craft to neutral buoyancy, or a position floating just below the surface of the water. The pilot of the craft turned a hand-operated vertical screw propeller (C) to drive the craft deeper. To surface, the pilot reversed the process. When the pilot stopped turning the vertical propeller, the *Turtle* returned to neutral buoyancy. The pilot then used a hand pump to empty the ballast tanks, making the craft lighter and returning it to the surface.

A hand-operated horizontal propeller (D) moved the *Turtle* forward. By reversing the direction of the propeller, the pilot could also drive the craft backward.

Bushnell equipped the *Turtle* with a rudder (E) for steering. He also designed a depth gauge (F), so the pilot could tell how far beneath the surface he was.

The *Turtle* contained only enough air for its pilot to remain underwater for thirty minutes. For longer voyages, Bushnell built two ventilator pipes (G) into the top of the craft. The pipes protruded above the surface of the water when the *Turtle* was slightly submerged. One pipe let fresh air in; the other let foul air out. Both were equipped with valves that automatically closed to keep water out.

pipes allowed air in while the viewing port was above water and kept water out while the vessel was submerged.

For its time the *Turtle* was a sophisticated device. It was a hand-powered machine, but unlike van Drebbel's boatload of oarsmen, the *Turtle* only needed a crew of one. That one person had a lot of work to do, however. The small craft, which measured only 7.5 feet long by 8 feet deep by 4 feet wide, had two screw-shaped, hand-cranked propellers. One propeller was mounted on the front and moved the sub forward and backward. The other was mounted on the top of the hull and helped the sub dive and ascend. As in van Drebbel's boat, water did most of the work in submerging and raising the *Turtle*. But the pilot of Bushnell's boat had a lot more control. A number of hand-and-foot-operated valves and pumps allowed the pilot to control the flow of water in and out of the ballast tank. In an emergency the pilot could detach a cone-shaped, lead weight mounted on the bottom of the hull, and the boat would quickly rise.

As if the pilot did not already have enough to do, he also had to operate the *Turtle*'s single weapon by hand. Bushnell's sub carried a 150-pound gunpowder bomb with a clockwork detonator. The bomb was anchored to the enemy ship's hull with the help of a hand-cranked drill located on the conning tower. The pilot's task was to maneuver the *Turtle* under an enemy warship's hull, drill into the hull (a difficult task, since all ship's hulls at that time were covered with copper plates to protect against mollusks that ate wood), anchor the bomb, set the fuse, detach the drill bit that held the bomb in place, and move away before the bomb exploded.

Maneuvering the sub was a challenge in itself. Although the pilot could see where he was going while the viewing port was above water, he was nearly blind once he submerged more than a few feet. Water, unless it is extremely clear, blocks most light. Bushnell provided a few primitive navigation devices, including a compass and a barometer that doubled as a depth gauge. The inventor used pieces of fox fire, a fungus that glows in the dark, to mark out the dial of the compass and the float in the depth gauge. However, he soon found out that the life of the fungus, which dies in very cold environments, restricted the sub's operations to spring, summer, and early fall.

The *Turtle*'s Test

Bushnell finished building and testing his *Turtle* in the summer of 1776, when the colonies broke their ties with Great Britain and established themselves as the United States of America. The British military responded rapidly, blockading ports and massing troops to quell this colonial uprising. In one of Great Britain's biggest shows of force, more than 350 warships blockaded New York Bay in July 1776. The flagship of this force, the HMS (His Majesty's Ship) *Eagle*, was one of the most heavily armed ships in the Royal Navy. It was a tempting target for the *Turtle*, which had already impressed a number of colonial leaders, including George Washington, in a demonstration of its abilities.

Over the course of six weeks American soldiers hauled the *Turtle* from Connecticut to the southern tip of Manhattan Island. The sub arrived late in the afternoon of September 5. For the next few hours its attendants tested the

The British fleet advances toward New York Bay unaware that its flagship, the Eagle, *is about to become the target of the world's first submarine attack.*

craft and fitted it with its bomb. Then, early in the morning of September 6 a boat towed the *Turtle* to a point just north of the *Eagle*. The sub and its pilot, Sergeant Ezra Lee, were then left to carry out the mission.

The attack on the *Eagle*—the first submarine attack on a surface warship—was truly a turning point in military history. But it also was the first failed submarine attack on a surface warship. With just the stubby conning tower and a few inches of the hull above water, the *Turtle* started moving toward its target. As Lee looked out the conning tower's window, he discovered that he was moving much faster than he had planned. Military planners had miscalculated the tide in New York Bay. The tide was carrying the little boat out to sea. Before Lee could correct his position, the *Turtle* had floated past its target. The unlucky sergeant was forced to turn the forward propeller in reverse for a full hour just to hold a position near the *Eagle*.

Lee finally reached his position beneath the *Eagle* just as dawn was begin-

ning to break, two and a half hours after starting on his mission. He judged that he had just enough time to attach the bomb, set the fuse, and make his escape before the sky grew light enough for the ship's watchmen to spot him. However, the drill failed to pierce the hull. Lee later wrote that he had accidentally positioned the drill right under a bar of iron that connected the *Eagle*'s rudder to the ship's stern. Though it could go through soft copper sheeting, the drill could not pierce iron. As he tried to move the sub to a new position, Lee accidentally let the sub slip out from under the hull and surface in the light of the rising sun.

Again Lee found fortune in the midst of his bad luck, for no one on the ship spotted him. He tried to steer toward American-held territory, but a malfunction in the compass sent him right toward a British fortress on Governor's Island. Lee later reported that more than four hundred British soldiers witnessed his advance on the fort and that about twenty soldiers set out in a barge to capture him. Hoping to blow rified the British sailors. The fleet scattered and many ships collided, leaving Lee free to escape and return to Manhattan Island.

Despite this psychological victory, neither the *Turtle* nor Bushnell were ever heard of after the attack. Bushnell himself apparently felt deeply embarrassed that the *Turtle* had not been able to sink its intended target. Soon after the attack he moved away from his Connecticut farm and changed his name, trying to avoid recognition for his work for the rest of his life.

The Challenge Continues

Although the attack failed, military planners realized that the submarine could be a powerful tool of war. A blockading fleet would not be able to protect itself against the silent appoach of an enemy submarine. Other inventors—not just part-time tinkerers, but experienced engineers—looked at ways of improving on the methods that Bushnell and earlier sub builders had used.

Robert Fulton, the inventor of the first successful steamboat, experimented

Robert Fulton, best known for his steamboats, developed a human-powered submarine that used a hand-cranked propeller for moving underwater.

up his pursuers, Lee triggered the fuse and let the bomb loose. The soldiers in the boat saw the bomb and veered away. The bomb blew up in the bay without sinking any ships, but the explosion ter-

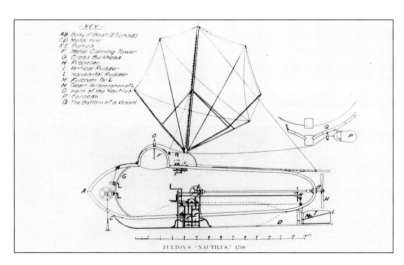

Fulton's Nautilus *could travel more than a mile underwater but was unable to sink slow-moving ships.*

around 1800 with a copper-hulled submarine. His submarine used a sail for long-distance travel on the surface and a hand-cranked, two-bladed propeller at the rear for maneuvering underwater. Like the *Turtle*, Fulton's *Nautilus* used a drill to anchor a bomb to the hull of a ship. Unlike Bushnell's sub, the *Nautilus* had a long, cigar-shaped main hull and looked remarkably like many modern submarines. Using a tank of compressed air, it could support a three-person crew for up to four hours at twenty-five feet below the water's surface. The *Nautilus* could travel a little more than a mile—not a great distance, but a significant achievement for the time. Its usefulness as a weapon of war was questionable, however. It sank a few stationary target ships during practice attack runs but could not catch up and sink even slow-moving targets.

The experiences of the *Turtle* and the *Nautilus*, and other early submarines, proved that inventors had much work to do before submarines would become menacing weapons. Inventors busied themselves with trying to lengthen time underwater, finding better ways to descend and ascend, and developing an efficient method of power.

A German artillery corporal named Wilhelm Bauer thought he had reached most of these goals in 1850 when he built an iron-hulled submarine he called the *Brandtaucher*, or *Sea Diver*. Bauer's vessel had a propeller at the stern powered by two crewmen walking on a treadmill. It also had a heavy weight that slid fore and aft along a track to keep the sub level while underwater. This system, Bauer thought,

An artist's conception of Wilhelm Bauer's Brandtaucher *firing its weapons at a warship during a test. When the* Brandtaucher *went against Denmark's fleet in 1850, its strange appearance frightened the Dutch into retreat.*

CSS *HUNLEY*

Soldiers keep watch over the CSS Hunley.

One of the most notorious of the nineteenth century human-powered submarines went into service during the American Civil War. The CSS (Confederate States Ship) *Hunley* was supposed to be the Confederacy's great weapon against Union warships. By 1863 the Union navy was successfully blockading the South's major trading ports from Virginia to the mouth of the Mississippi River. The Confederate government desperately needed to free these ports in order to receive the foreign goods and money needed to maintain its war against the Union. It hoped that the *Hunley*, designed by an engineer named Horace L. Hunley, would be able to sneak up on Union warships and, with a gunpowder bomb mounted on the end of a spar, blow them up.

In reality the *Hunley* was an almost-perfect death trap. It looked like a flat-sided railroad tank car with a propeller at the stern, or back, and the gunpowder bomb at the bow, or front. The two hatches built into the top of the hull were so close to the waterline that the roughly thirty-foot-long craft was continually swamped by waves and the wakes of surface vessels during its trial runs. The hatches had to be kept open to keep from suffocating the eight men who turned the propeller shaft, as well as the one or two officers who steered the craft. As a result of numerous swampings, thirteen men, including Horace Hunley, drowned in the sub before it ever saw action.

The *Hunley* itself had a short life. The only time the *Hunley* sank an enemy warship, it sank itself at the same time. On February 17, 1864, the sub crept up on the new steam-powered Union warship USS (United States Ship) *Housatonic*, which was part of a blockade near Charleston, South Carolina. The *Hunley* crew exploded its bomb right at the warship's waterline. But the *Housatonic* sank so fast that the *Hunley* could not get out of the way. The sinking warship trapped the small sub under its hull, carrying its crew to their deaths. The *Hunley* was one of the last human-powered submarines built for combat. If nothing else, its fate proved that human power was not enough to run a successful fighting submarine.

Theodore Nordenfelt's steam-powered submarine captured in a photograph that was taken in Stockholm, Sweden.

would balance the boat by keeping it from tipping at the bow or stern.

The *Brandtaucher*'s first test came soon after it was built. In 1850 Germany and Denmark were at war to decide who would claim a region covering two small countries, Schleswig and Holstein. A Dutch fleet was blockading the harbor of Kiel, where Germany had set up a government for the region. The *Brandtaucher* proved to be the key to breaking the blockade. Though it was slow and unarmed, the sight of the *Brandtaucher* entering the harbor was enough to scare off the Dutch fleet, which withdrew to the open sea.

This was the *Brandtaucher*'s only success. After chasing away the Dutch fleet, Bauer began testing his sub in the harbor to see how deep it could dive. On one of these dives a couple of faulty rivets popped out of some hull plates and let a stream of water into the crew compartment. As the water flooded the sub, the bow dipped down and the balancing weight slid all the way forward. This sent the *Brandtaucher* into a crash dive, which ended sixty feet below the sur-

face, with the sub stuck nose-first in the harbor floor. Bauer and the two crew members escaped the damaged vessel and survived.

Bauer later built a more successful submarine, the *Diable-Marin* (*Sea Devil*), which he sold to Russia in 1855. This craft made more than one hundred successful dives, including one dive carrying a brass band that played an underwater concert to celebrate the coronation of Czar Alexander II. The music filtered up through the water to the fleet of ships packed in to hear this marvelous serenade.

The Way Is Set

Bauer's two vessels seemed to herald a half century of intense work to perfect the devices originally built by van Drebbel, Bushnell, and Fulton. His craft were also among the last attempts to build human-powered submarines. Inventors finally had come to realize that human beings alone could not handle the task of operating *and* powering a successful submarine. Accordingly, submarine designers started using a variety of mechanical means to run their boats. They built motors powered by tanks of compressed air, by steam, and by electricity, with varying results.

Electricity and Steam

In France in 1863 Simeon Borgeois and Charles-Marie Brun built the *Plongeur* (the *Diver*), a 140-foot-long submarine powered by compressed air. Nearly twenty years later another French inventor built the first of two electrically powered submarines. In 1878 English inventor G. Garrett and Norwegian engineer Theodore Nordenfelt each built successful steam-powered submarines, which stored steam that was generated on the surface for power underwater. Seven years later Garrett and Nordenfelt teamed up to build the *Nordenfelt I*, a sixty-ton steam submarine they sold to Greece. Between 1886 and 1890 two other French inventors, Dupuy de Lome and Gustave Zédé, also built a pair of electric subs—the *Gymnote* and the *Gustave Zede*—which operated as part of the French navy until the early

1900s.

Most of these submarines were incomplete vessels, however. As advanced as they were, the French electric submarines could go only as fast and as far as their batteries would allow. They had to return to their berths before their cells ran out of power. The steam-powered submarines of Garrett and Nordenfelt were more powerful, but their hot boilers made their crews feel as if they were working in a sauna. Submerging was a twelve-to-fifteen-minute process, most of it waiting for the boilers to cool down. And once the subs were underwater, they could run for only about ten miles before they ran out of stored steam. The early compressed air subs, such as the *Plongeur* and a few Russian-built craft, had even more limited ranges and lower speeds than the electric subs of France.

What was needed was an engine, or combination of engines, that would allow submarines to travel as fast underwater as they could on the surface, with much faster speeds and greater ranges than were available. Finally, at the end of the century two American inventors would develop submarines that would show this type of self-sufficiency.

Submarines from New Jersey

By the end of the 1860s most of the world's naval powers were experimenting with submarines. Virtually the only seagoing nation without an official submarine program was the United States. In 1872 the U.S. Navy bought a human-powered submarine called the *Intelligent Whale* from a New Jersey inventor, Oliver Halstead. Though Halstead's initial demonstration for the navy was a success, the *Intelligent Whale* gained fame as the submarine that drowned thirty-nine men during its next three dives. After those disasters, the U.S. government was reluctant to trust anyone who claimed to have found a way to travel underwater. But reluctance gave way to practical

needs as the twentieth century dawned. Because of two other New Jersey inventors, each with his own idea of how a submarine should operate, the United States joined other naval powers in building submarine fleets that would forever change warfare at sea.

Pointing the Way

The first British and American submarines were patterned on the designs of an Irish schoolteacher who hoped his ideas would be put to use against the British navy. While working as a teacher in Dundalk, Ireland, John Holland had

A successful demonstration convinced the U.S. Navy to buy the human-powered Intelligent Whale *submarine, but it turned out to be an unworthy underwater vessel. The navy's faith in submarines was badly shaken after the submarine claimed thirty-nine lives.*

The U.S. Civil War battle between the Virginia *and the* Monitor *convinced John Holland of the benefits of building a metal-hulled submarine that could attack unseen and without warning.*

read newspaper accounts of the sinking of the USS *Housatonic* and of the battle between the Union and Confederate ironclad warships, the *Monitor* and the *Virginia* (formerly the *Merrimac*). Holland thought that these two battles were signposts pointing the way toward the future of naval combat. He believed the future lay in metal-hulled submersible warships that could hide in any of the world's seas.

Holland drew up plans for a one-man, cigar-shaped, human-powered submersible attack craft with air tanks made of oiled silk. He hoped Ireland could use his vessel in its ongoing battle with Great Britain over British rule. But Holland had neither the time nor the money to complete his work and, for several years, the project languished.

Holland immigrated to the United States in 1873, bringing his drawings with him. When he arrived in the United States, Holland took a job as a teacher in Paterson, New Jersey. As part of his work he tutored students at his home. One day in 1874 one of Holland's students saw his teacher's drawings. The boy told his father, who was a

friend of the secretary of the navy, about Holland's designs. Because the man knew that the navy was looking for practical submarine designs, he encouraged Holland to send them to the navy. Holland, eager to have his designs accepted, spent almost a year refining them before sending them in.

Subs for the Fenians

The navy by that time had lost its patience with human-powered submarines, thanks to its experience with the *Intelligent Whale*. When Holland sent in his plans in 1875, they were rejected by a navy officer who, according to naval historian Robert F. Burgess, said that "no one with any sense would go underwater in such a contraption in the first place." But John Holland's brother Michael, who had also moved to America, knew of another group that might be interested in Holland's plans. Michael was a member of the Fenian Society, a group of Irish immigrants who raised money to support the Irish rebellion against England. The Fenians maintained a "skirmishing fund" for various undercover projects, including the development of weapons. Michael Holland knew that he could get the Fenians to pay John to build them a sub they could use against the British navy. It took a while for Michael to convince the Fenians to meet with John, but in the winter of 1876 John Holland began working for the Irish rebels.

The first submarine Holland built, named the *Holland I*, was only about as big as a modern pickup truck. It looked like a riveted metal cigar with four flat sides that tapered toward a two-bladed propeller in the rear. It had a short conning tower, which looked like a fat-stemmed mushroom with a series of viewports for surface and shallow underwater navigation. The sub's small size and ungainly appearance led Paterson residents to call it an iron coffin.

The sub was designed to dive with the aid of two rectangular metal planks, called diving planes. The diving planes were mounted horizontally near the bow, and used to help push the bow below the surface. Holland abandoned the idea of building a human-powered sub, settling instead on an iron-hulled craft with a gasoline engine. The engine was to power the sub on the surface and underwater. To keep the burning gasoline from using up the crew's air while submerged, the engine fed off a tank of compressed air. A pipe was attached to the engine to send exhaust fumes outside the hull through a one-way valve.

Injured Pride

Holland had enough problems with the *Holland I* to justify its nickname. In its first two test runs water poured into its

Problems with the Holland I *did not discourage John Holland. He later designed a successful gasoline-powered submarine, the* Fenian Ram.

hull. Each time, the sub sank as soon as it hit the water. Holland was deeply embarrassed when his marvelous invention sank in full view of the members of the Fenian Society. Although the sinkings injured Holland's pride, nobody was hurt in either episode. The Paterson newspaper added to Holland's discomfort, congratulating him on his success in building a self-wrecking boat.

The problem, Holland discovered, was faulty rivets. But when the rivets were replaced, Holland found that the gasoline engine did not work. Neither Holland nor any of his assistants could find the source of the engine's trouble. But with the Fenians becoming impatient to see some results for all the money they had spent (about four thousand dollars at the time), Holland needed to demonstrate the sub's abilities soon. Finally he thought to run a steam hose from a steamboat's boiler through the conning tower and into the *Holland I*'s engine. The steam line gave the engine the power it needed to turn the propeller, though the sub would not be able to cruise far from the surface vessel. Even so, the *Holland I* was able to submerge, travel underwater at a depth of twelve feet, and return to the surface under power. The Fenians were impressed by the demonstration.

The *Fenian Ram*

Though he had finally succeeded, Holland decided to abandon the *Holland I* and build a better one in its place. He designed a new gasoline engine and made plans for a weapon that used compressed air to fire explosives at enemy ships while underwater. Holland convinced the Fenians to pay for the larger, redesigned submarine, saying it would be a more effective weapon against the Royal Navy. To keep the *Holland I* from falling into the hands of British spies, he sank it in fourteen feet of water under one of Paterson's bridges.

Holland made his new sub a much superior vessel to the *Holland I*. The thirty-one-foot-long craft even looked like a success—Holland had smoothed the design of the hull, giving it a blimp-like shape that could easily push through the water. It was cramped inside, however, measuring only six feet wide and a little more than seven feet from the keel, or hull bottom, to the top of the hull. Most of this space was taken up by the ballast tanks, motor, the propulsion gear, and the two compressed air tanks fore and aft. In addition to providing air for the crew, the

air tanks blew water out of the sub's ballast tanks. This method of releasing ballast was a radical change from the hand-operated or mechanical water pumps that had been used in the past. The air tanks allowed the submarine to return to the surface even if its pumps or motor failed. The compressed air also charged an air-powered gun that could fire a nine-inch-diameter missile.

Although John Holland's work was supposed to be a secret, his inventions were popular news in New England. A New York reporter, Blakely Hall, had tried without success to talk with Holland about his second submarine. The Fenians had tried to hide their identities behind a number of companies that supposedly were building the submarine for commercial purposes. But Hall managed to break through these layers of deception and find out the true identity of the submarine's patrons, whom he exposed in an article in the *New York Sun*. And while Holland thought he would simply call his craft the *Holland II*, Hall gave it a name that described its true purpose—the *Fenian Ram*.

Unlike the *Holland I*, the *Fenian Ram* was a success from its first test dive, this time in New York Harbor. It dove and ascended with no trouble and traveled underwater at nine knots, or roughly ten and a half miles an hour. Still, the *Fenian Ram* was limited in how far it could travel and how deep it could dive.

Holland figured that the best and least expensive way to improve his design would be to experiment with a smaller sub. He had one built. At sixteen feet long it measured about half the size of the *Ram*. The members of the Fenian Society, however, were losing interest in the inventor's unending string of improvements and with the ex-

DIVING AND SURFACING

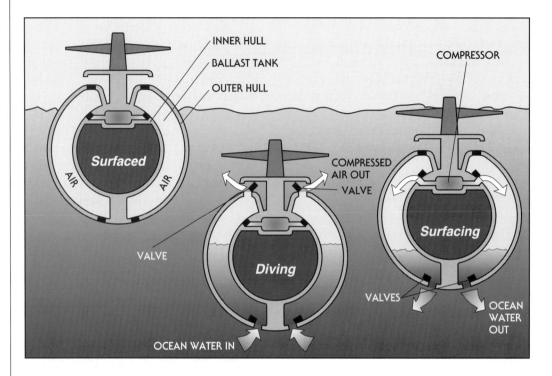

The modern submarine relies on compressed air and ocean water for diving and surfacing. The submarine expels compressed air and draws in water to dive. The submarine draws in compressed air and expels ocean water to surface.

The intake and outflow of air and water occurs within the submarine's ballast tanks, located between the inner and outer hulls. In the surfaced position, that is, when the submarine is floating or buoyant, the ballast tanks contain compressed air. When the compressed air is released through valves at the top of the ballast tanks, ocean water is drawn through the bottom of the ballast tanks. Since the water in the tank weighs more than the air it displaces, the submarine becomes heavier and sinks.

To surface, the process is reversed. The compressor pumps air into the ballast tanks. At the same time, valves at the bottom of the tanks are opened. Pressure from the compressed air forces the water through the valves and out of the ballast tanks, causing the submarine to become lighter and allowing it to rise.

pense of paying for them. The Fenians wanted to sink British warships. They ran out of patience, stole both the *Fenian Ram* and the smaller sub, and towed them toward the port of New Haven, Connecticut.

The smaller sub sank during the trip because the Fenians forgot to close the hatch. The *Fenian Ram* was used for a couple of practice attack runs in New

Haven's harbor, though without submerging and without firing its gun. Complaints from captains and shipowners convinced the New Haven harbor master to order the boat out of the water as a menace to navigation.

Simon Lake's Subs of Exploration

As John Holland looked for a way to continue his submarine experiments, a New Jersey boy named Simon Lake dreamed about exploring the ocean depths. Lake was a troubled child, the type who broke windows for fun, angered his teachers, and beat up other students. On the other hand, he had an amazing ability to make or fix any sort of mechanical device. When he was nine, he took apart a sewing machine and rebuilt it better than it had been before. And he surprised his family by building a working watch from a box of jumbled watch parts. But this ability did not endear Lake to many people outside his family. Even family members saw little future for him.

When he was eleven, however, Lake came across Jules Verne's novel, *Twenty Thousand Leagues Under the Sea.* Lake was fascinated by Verne's tale of the *Nautilus,* an electrically powered submarine, and its creator, Captain Nemo. After reading the book Lake decided that, more than anything else, he wanted to build submarines. He studied Verne's description of the *Nautilus* and began thinking up ways to improve the design. He timed how long he could breathe the air in an overturned canoe and began reading everything he could find about shipbuilding and underwater construction. He even drew up plans

for an air lock that would allow divers to enter and leave the submarine while it was submerged.

In 1883, when he was seventeen, Lake left school to learn the practical side of mechanics in his father's New Jersey iron foundry. There, he honed the creative skills he had been born with. Over the next ten years he drew up plans for the submarine he wished to build. Unlike Holland, Lake designed a blimp-shaped submarine that submerged and ascended horizontally, or on an even keel, rather than diving or surfacing nose-first. Besides the air lock, which Lake felt was vital for underwater exploration, his submarine had

An illustration from Jules Verne's Twenty Thousand Leagues Under the Sea *depicts* Nautilus *crew members fighting off the fierce attack of a giant octopus.*

Simon Lake used his mechanical know-how to design submarines that submerged and ascended with an even motion rather than diving or rising nose first.

another unusual feature: wheels. Two ten-foot-wide, gear-toothed, metal wheels were mounted on each side of the hull, and a smaller, pivoting wheel was mounted on a post at the stern. Lake thought of his submarine as a mobile research base that could follow divers as they explored the sea floor.

The only thing that kept Lake from building his dream sub—which he called the *Argonaut*—was money. But by 1893 the U.S. Navy again was interested in building submarines, provided no one tried to sell them any human-powered disasters like the *Intelligent Whale*. Lake learned that the navy was sponsoring a design competition to find an engineer who could build a fighting submarine. Lake thought his submarine plans, with a few changes, would show the navy that he was the best candidate for the job. Lake had no idea of the strength and experience of one of his competitors—John Holland.

Holland's *Holland*

The competition to build the sub, which the navy dubbed the *Plunger*, followed a simple process. Each inventor—Holland, Lake, and a Chicago man named George Baker—traveled to the office of the secretary of the navy, discussed his ideas with the design committee, and left a copy of his plans. Lake's design, with its wheels and its diver's air lock, was apparently too unconventional even for the unconventional craft the navy wanted to build. In addition, Holland had already built three submarines, the *Fenian Ram*, the *Holland I*, and the small submarine the Fenians sank. Holland received the contract. Outraged that the government had turned down what he believed to be a clearly superior vessel, Lake decided to build it anyway and prove the government experts wrong.

Getting the *Plunger* contract ended up being no great victory for Holland. At first, the $150,000 project seemed to cement Holland's future as a submarine designer. He founded his own firm, the John P. Holland Torpedo Boat Company, and made plans to build the sub according to the plans that had won the competition. But the navy's submarine design committee had its own ideas of what features the *Plunger* should have. It wanted the boat to have a high surface speed to pursue and attack warships, and it wanted the sub to run nearly as fast underwater. It insisted that the *Plunger* be built with a steam engine, though Holland said that a gasoline engine would give the sub greater speed and keep the crew's work space cooler.

A few months later the committee decided to take Holland's advice, although it ordered Holland to install a separate engine for each of the sub's three propellers. To keep the contract Holland had to agree to these changes, but he predicted that the boat would be a failure. He was proved right in 1896, when the newly completed boat showed it could not even keep a straight course.

While building the *Plunger*, Holland had started work on the sub he knew the committee should have asked for. Holland launched the new sub in May 1897 and spent most of the next year testing and tinkering with the craft to make sure it would perform flawlessly when he showed it to navy officials.

The fifty-three-foot-long boat was a masterpiece worth fussing over. Holland had taken the revolutionary step of giving it two separate power sources, a gasoline engine for cruising on the surface, and a battery-driven electric motor for underwater operations. The gasoline engine gave the boat the speed

it would need (up to eight knots) to pursue its targets, while the battery-driven motor eliminated both the heat buildup and the danger of running out of air while submerged. In addition, the gas engine powered a generator that not only recharged the batteries, but also provided light for the sub's crew. Electric lights must have been a true luxury to Holland. In his other subs he had been forced to rely on the dim light that filtered through the conning tower portholes, only briefly lighting an oil lantern to check his depth gauges and compasses.

The sub's hull, like the *Fenian Ram*'s, looked like a fat cigar, with rudders, or steering mechanisms, and diving planes mounted just forward of the propeller. A short conning tower supported the main, and only, hatch. There was virtually no other structure on the hull. Holland was adamant about keeping the hull clear of anything that would increase drag, or slow the boat down, while it was underwater. When a coworker suggested that the navy admirals might prefer a less un-

John Holland's Plunger *did not live up to expectations. But the fault lay with the navy, which ordered changes in Holland's design.*

conventional design, Holland replied "I shall not give them a deck to strut about on!"

The submarine's weapons were equally advanced. By the late 1890s a new type of weapon, the self-propelled torpedo, had been developed for use at sea. These weapons were referred to as Whitehall torpedoes, because they had been invented by engineers at the British navy armory at Whitehall, on the southeastern coast of England. Holland equipped his vessel with three Whitehall torpedoes, which were fired from an air-powered torpedo tube in the bow. Some news accounts from the time also suggest that the boat had two other weapons, a "dynamite torpedo" that was fired from a gun at the rear of the craft,

and an "aerial torpedo" (essentially a mortar) that fired a shell from the top of the hull.

Holland's newest creation impressed every visitor who came to see it during May and April 1898. Theodore Roosevelt, the assistant secretary of the navy at the time, wrote to the secretary: "I think the Holland submarine should be purchased. . . . Sometimes she doesn't work perfectly, but often she does, and I don't think in the present emergency we can afford to let her slip (by)." The emergency the future president referred to was the war with Spain that everybody in the nation, and certainly everybody in the nation's capitol, knew was coming.

Despite these encouraging reports,

The USS Holland *looked like a fat cigar. But with its new self-propelled torpedoes it became a powerful weapon.*

STEERING

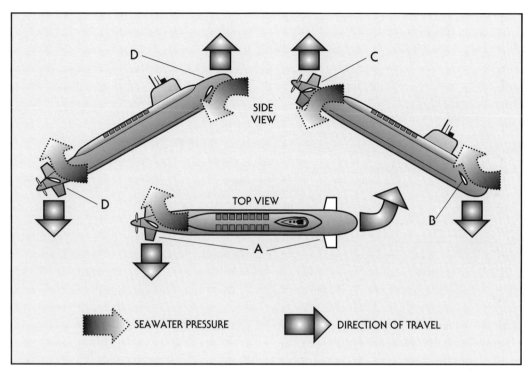

Like conventional ships, submarines use a vertical rear rudder to steer the vessel left and right. Unlike conventional ships, however, submarines must also control their movement up and down through the water. To do this, submarines use two sets of horizontal rudders mounted at each end of the hull. These rudders are known as diving planes (A). The pressure from seawater moving across the diving planes controls the submarine's movement. To dive, for example, the forward diving plane is angled downward (B). Pressure against the top of the diving plane forces the bow of the submarine deeper into the water. At the same time, the rear diving plane (C) is angled upward. Pressure on the bottom side of the diving plane forces the stern of the submarine upward, increasing the angle of the dive.

To move upward, the position of the diving planes is reversed. The forward diving plane is angled upward (D). Pressure against the bottom side of the diving plane pushes the bow of the submarine upward. The rear diving plane is angled downward (E). Pressure against the top side of the diving plane forces the stern of the submarine downward, increasing the angle of the submarine's ascent.

the Spanish-American War came and went without Holland's submarine. In March 1900 Holland decided to force the government's hand. He invited members of Congress and navy officers—including Admiral George Dewey, who had defeated the Spanish navy's Philippines fleet—to a demonstration of the submarine. Dewey said that, with two of Holland's boats, the otherwise antiquated Spanish navy could have fought off his entire squadron of modern American cruisers and destroyers. A month later the navy bought the submarine and christened it the USS *Holland*.

For the next three years Congress debated whether or not the nation needed any more submarines. Holland, impatient to continue his work and in need of money, searched outside the United States for other customers. He sold a larger version of the *Holland*, the *Fulton*, to the Russian Imperial Navy, which was preparing for a war against Japan. He also sold five boats to Japan, though neither side ended up using the craft in the 1904 Russo-Japanese War.

The U.S. government ordered six more Holland submarines in 1903. The navy also asked Holland to rebuild the old *Plunger*, which had been sitting in a storage berth since 1898. In an ironic twist of fate, Holland went on to design five submarines for Great Britain's Royal Navy, which he had once hoped to destroy. Though many high-ranking officers condemned the submarine as "damned un-English" and the moral equivalent of seventeenth-century pirate ships, more reasonable minds saw that submarines would play an important role in future sea battles. The British government paid Holland's company a licensing fee to let an English firm, Vickers, build the craft.

A Sad End

Sadly, Holland was to have little joy at seeing his submarines go to work in fleets around the world. He designed one last submarine, the *Octopus*, which won another U.S. Navy competition and which pushed the new technology of submarine design even farther. While he was doing this, his partners in the Holland Torpedo Boat Company—later renamed the Electric Boat Company—took over the business, leaving him little more than a figurehead with a salary of ninety dollars a week. By the time Holland realized what had happened, it was too late to do anything about it. De-

Holland's Fulton *at sea. In need of money and eager to continue designing submarines, Holland sold the* Fulton *to the Russian Imperial Navy, which was preparing for the Russo-Japanese War.*

The Octopus, *a technological advancement in submarine design, won a U.S. Navy competition. It was Holland's last submarine.*

pressed and discouraged by his partners' betrayal, Holland retired from his submarine career and spent the last ten years of his life studying the principles of flight. He died in 1914.

Lake Takes the Lead

Though Simon Lake had lost the U.S. Navy contract to Holland, his submarine-building business blossomed. After losing the *Plunger* contract, Lake decided to raise the money for his sub, the *Argonaut*, on his own. First he needed to prove that his ideas would work. He borrowed money from relatives and built a box-shaped wood-and-canvas submersible, complete with three wheels and an air lock. Together with his cousin and assistant, Bert Champion, Lake christened the craft *Argonaut Jr.* The vessel was only fourteen feet long by seven feet high. It had a hand-powered propeller and a bicycle's pedal-and-chain assembly for turning the two main wheels. A tank of compressed air pressurized the small air lock in the bow of the boat. When the air pressure in the lock was the same as the water pressure outside the hull, Lake could open the outer hatch, located on the bottom of the hull, without letting any water in.

The *Argonaut Jr.* proved that Lake's designs could work. He gave public demonstrations of the little wooden craft to build interest and support for his next project, the creation of the Lake Submarine Company, which would build the *Argonaut*. He sold stock in the fledgling firm to his family and neighbors and other investors.

Like the USS *Holland*, the *Argonaut* used a gasoline engine to enable it to

Though some government officials were interested in Lake's design, Holland's submarines had more support in Congress, which was debating whether or not the United States needed any submarines at all. Like Holland, Lake looked to other nations for buyers, eventually selling the *Protector* to the Russians. He also moved to Russia to supervise the construction of four more boats. From Russia he went to Austria, where he built two submarines, and then to Germany, where he sold plans for a submarine to a branch of the Krupp industrial firm. Unfortunately, Lake did not register his designs with the German government, which allowed Krupp to build and improve on Lake's designs without paying him any royalties.

Annoyed by this dishonesty, Lake re-

Unable to win a government contract, Simon Lake raised money on his own to build submarines. With flags raised, Lake's Argonaut *gets underway about 1898.*

A view of the Argonaut's *engine room. A gasoline engine propelled the* Argonaut *on the surface and underwater.*

run on the surface and to charge the batteries that propelled the boat underwater. Unlike Holland's boat, the *Argonaut* and Lake's later submarines dove and surfaced on an even keel, rather than by forcing the nose up or down. The *Argonaut* also had enough air to stay underwater for at least ten hours.

Despite these features no one wanted to buy the *Argonaut*, nor did anyone in America want Lake's next submarine, the *Protector*, which he launched in 1902. The *Protector* looked more like Holland's designs, although it still had the Lake wheels and air lock. The *Protector* also had three torpedo tubes, two in the bow and one in the stern.

turned to America around 1910 and tried once again to sell a submarine to his own country. Navy officials refused even to examine Lake's newest boat, the *Simon Lake X*, which Lake then sold to the Russian government. A year later, Lake finally made his sale to the U.S. government. Lake offered to build a 161-foot-long submarine that could carry six torpedoes and a crew of twenty-four—all at his own expense, provided Congress would take a look at the craft when it was finished. This submarine, the *Seal*, was larger and could travel farther than any previous submarine, and was able to plant mines and cut mine cables while submerged. The *Seal* was so impressive that Congress bought it immediately. Its commissioning in October 1912 marked the beginning of a thirty-three year relationship between Lake and the U.S. Navy, which ended only upon Lake's death in 1945.

The work of Holland and Lake set the stage for the development of all other submarines. The combination of gasoline, and later diesel, engines with electric motors would be standard in every submarine from 1903 until the nuclear-powered USS *Nautilus* was launched in 1954. While the wheels on the first few submarines Lake invented would not become a standard design feature, his method of even-keel dives and ascents would replace Holland's unsettling nose-first method. On the other hand, Holland's original blimp-like hull designs—abandoned in favor of a wedge-shaped bow that allowed a faster surface speed—would reappear fifty years later in a new generation of subs. All in all, the Holland and Lake submarines were the first truly practical submarines and capped more than three hundred years of inventing and reinventing. Now it was up to the navies of the world to find out how best to use these new vessels.

Unseen Tools of War

The navies of the world spent the ten years before World War I trying to find a place for submarines in their fleets. The new technology was utterly different from any other warship that had ever been in service. At first, simply keeping submarine crews alive was a challenge. Although these early subs were successful, there were limits on how fast, how far, and how deep they could go. For instance, Great Britain's first submarine, which the Royal Navy called *Holland I*, was supposedly built to travel up to one hundred feet below the surface. Tests of the hull in the 1980s, however, showed that water pressure would have crushed it at sixty feet.

Other problems had to be overcome as well. One of the biggest problems was the risk of battery explosions. The batteries stored electricity gener-ated by the gasoline engines to power the boat underwater. But early batteries gave off lots of hydrogen, an explosive gas that could be ignited by a hot pipe or a spark from a battery cable. The battery problem was worsened by the possibility of an explosion's cracking or punching a hole in the hull. Although holes could sometimes be patched, if water reached the battery compartment, the mixture of sea water and battery acid would form lethal chlorine gas, which could kill the entire crew.

The dangers of submarine travel were magnified by the inexperience of the first submarine crews. A simple mistake like opening the wrong valve could quickly send a submarine and its crew to the bottom of the sea. As there were no escape hatches or air locks in most of these early boats, such an event was

German crew members stand shoulder to shoulder in the engine room of their submarine. Early submarine crews endured dangerous conditions and the ever present risk of explosions.

DIESEL POWER

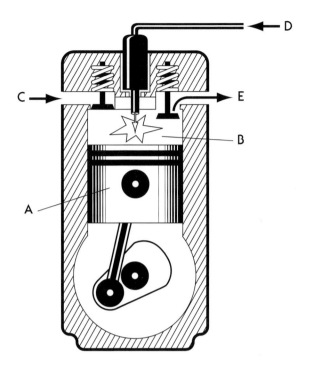

The gasoline engine provided the first practical means of propelling a submarine on and below the water's surface. But it quickly faded from favor with the introduction of the diesel engine. The diesel engine was simpler, safer, and more economical than the gasoline engine and it remained the primary means of propelling submarines until the arrival of nuclear power.

The diesel engine was invented in 1897 by a German engineer, Rudolf Diesel. Like the steam engine, the diesel engine works by moving a piston (A) up and down inside a cylinder (B).

As the piston moves down, it draws in air through the intake valve (C). When the intake valve closes, the piston moves up, compressing the air in the closed chamber. As the air is compressed, it heats up. At the moment of greatest compression and heat, a fuel injector (D) sprays a fine mist of heating oil into the cylinder. The superheated air ignites the fuel, creating an explosion inside the cylinder. The expanding gases from this explosion push the piston downward with tremendous force. The exhaust valve (E) opens, allowing the gases to escape from the chamber.

almost always fatal. Submarine captains sometimes also made serious mistakes. More than once a skipper grounded his craft on a beach or a reef while trying to navigate underwater. A captain who beached a surface ship probably would have been fired for incompetence. Submarine skippers, on the other hand, commanded less respect than their peers on surface ships and so routinely

Rough seas did not slow the powerful German U-boat. Its outer hull cut the waves like a fast-moving surface ship.

received no penalties for running their boats ashore. In fact, one young American sub commander who beached his vessel was commended for using the accident as an opportunity to clean off the submarine's hull.

Despite these problems most of the major naval powers rapidly learned how to make their submarines perform. Crews gradually caught on to the dangers and quirks of their boats. Many of the disastrous explosions stopped when sub builders began using diesel, rather than gasoline, engines. And captains learned how to keep their boats off the coastlines and in the water where they belonged.

Submarine Combat in World War I

By the start of World War I the world's submarine fleets were measured in the tens. In all, barely more than four hundred submarines were in use around the world. Most of these belonged to Great Britain, Germany, Russia, and the United States. Smaller naval powers like France, Italy, the Netherlands, and Norway eventually began building diesel-electric boats of their own, though they had to struggle at first to catch up with the larger nations. For a while these smaller nations had only a handful of submarines, many of them steam- or electric-powered craft from the 1890s.

Great Britain had one of the largest sub fleets: seventy-four boats that were refined versions of the original five Holland-style boats. The only major difference in the design of these subs was that the ballast tanks were attached to the outside of the hull, where they looked like two large saddlebags. Germany, on the other hand, had one of the smallest fleets, made up of only twenty submarines. However, these subs—called *Unterseebooten* (German for "undersea boats"), known as U-boats—had advanced far beyond the two submarines Simon Lake had built during his brief stay in Berlin, Germany's capital city.

The U-boats of World War I had an operating range of five thousand miles, with a surface cruising speed of eighteen knots an hour. Much of this speed and range came from the powerful diesel engines Germany had developed after the turn of the century. But the high performance also came from a significant advance in design: a secondary, or outer, hull. Shaped much like the hull of a surface ship, the outer hull surrounded the cigar-shaped pressure hull. The interior pressure hull, as its name implies, protected the crew and vital equipment from being crushed by the surrounding sea.

English and American submarines were built with just one hull separating the crew from the sea, with the ballast tanks mounted outside the hull like a pair of saddlebags. While this design was stable underwater, in most cases it made for uncomfortable surface travel if the sea was choppy. Since a submarine spent most of its time on the surface, diving only when an enemy ship or plane was sighted, it made sense to have an outside hull that cut the waves like a ship.

For all its technological advancement, however, the U-boat was an uncomfortable vessel to work in. Virtually every inch of the boat was designed for power and combat, with little or no concern for the comfort of the crew. Sailors slept in bunks crammed among torpedo tubes, in gaps between machinery, or wherever else they could find space. The officers had a slightly easier time. They were given narrow bunks in an otherwise empty passageway in the middle of the sub, usually just ahead of the captain's closet-sized cabin. Naval historian Douglas Botting, in his book *The U-boats*, describes other hardships U-boat crews had to put up with:

> On long patrols especially, crews lived in an atmosphere of increasing squalor. The heat was oppressive, the air stale and foul and reeking of bilge water, wet oilskins [raincoats], rubber boots, sweat, and diesel fumes so thick that a man's hair became a pitchy mire. The U-boat grew steadily damper from the intense condensation and the frequent leakage of water through the conning tower. Bunks smelled [moldy] and charts began to rot. A gray-green film of mildew coated shoes and shirts. Sausages sprouted luxurious coats of mold overnight.

Crews in the early submarines of other countries also had to face conditions like these. American submarine sailors nicknamed their craft "pig boats,"

Early submarines offered little living space for crew members. Discomfort was an accepted fact of life on a submarine.

a name that reflected their living conditions and their discomfort when their subs took to sea. Also, the nose-first diving and surfacing method in the early Holland submarines mimicked porpoises and dolphins, which sailors called "sea pigs."

Germany was the first nation to give submarines a major role in war, but the first U-boat action hardly seemed to show the threat that submarines would become in later years. As the German government declared war against Great Britain in July 1914, ten U-boats formed a forty-mile-long line across the North Sea and cruised toward the Orkney Islands in search of British warships. One of the U-boats sank after blundering into a mine field. Another was rammed and sunk by a British cruiser, the HMS *Birmingham*, after firing torpedoes at three battleships—and missing. The remaining eight U-boats slunk back to their base on the northwestern coast of Germany. In a further insult to German pride, the war's first submarine victim was a German cruiser, the *Hela*. The

Hela was sunk by a British submarine in the North Sea, near the U-boats' home base.

Two months later Germany's luck changed. In early September 1914 the German submarine U-21 sank a British cruiser (a fast, moderately armored warship) with one torpedo. (U-boats had no name; they were designated only by the letter *U* and a number.) Two weeks later, the U-9 sank three British cruisers—the HMS *Aboukir*, HMS *Cressy*, and HMS *Hogue*—off the coast of the Netherlands in less than an hour. The first officer of the U-9, Johannes Speis, later recalled how the *Cressy* looked as she sank:

> The giant with four funnels turned slowly over to port. Men climbed like ants over her sides and then, as she turned turtle completely, they ran about on her broad flat keel until, in a few minutes, she disappeared beneath the waves.

The men of the U-9 instantly became heroes in Germany and villains to the admirals of the Royal Navy, who were

After eight German U-boats failed to inflict any damage upon Great Britain's forces in 1914, the U-9 (pictured here) restored German pride by sinking three British cruisers.

The captain of the U-9, Otto Wedigen (seated third from left) became a hero after he and his crew sank three Royal Navy warships in 1914.

stunned at how fast they had lost three ships and 1,460 sailors. The commander of the U-9, Otto Wedigen, went on to become one of the great U-boat commanders of World War II.

A Clash with Tradition

Just as the new submarine technology was out of place in a traditional navy fleet, so too was it at odds with centuries of tradition surrounding combat at sea. This tradition demanded that warships follow certain rules that set out how and when single ships or war fleets could fight each other. According to these rules of war, merchant ships, merchant sailors, and civilian passengers were treated differently from warships and fighting sailors. Merchant ships could not be attacked without being challenged and searched beforehand to see if they were from an enemy nation or from a neutral country. A merchant ship's crew, as well as any passengers, had to be taken on board the enemy ship and transported to the nearest neutral port. The merchant ship could then be either sunk or captured as a prize of war, providing the attacking warship could spare enough officers and crew to make up a skeleton crew.

Attempts were made to force submarines to obey these rules. International treaties required a sub to surface near the merchant ship, fire one warning shot across the ship's bow, and send a small boarding party to check the ship's cargo and papers. The merchant ship's crew was obliged to return the courtesy by not attempting to fight back

A submarine crew fires at an enemy steamer in 1917. Submarines found it difficult to obey the rules of war created for warships.

against their captors and by not trying to signal friendly warships about the submarine's presence. Against enemy warships, however, these rules did not apply.

These codes of behavior, known as the rules of engagement, were all but impossible for U-boat crews to follow, although they tried their best at first. One month after the U-9's victory the U-17 claimed the first merchant ship sunk by a submarine—the *Glitra*, a British cargo ship. The U-17's captain followed the required procedure, firing a shot across the ship's bow and ordering its crew off before sinking it. Since there was no extra space in the submarine, the ship's crew was allowed to row away in lifeboats after receiving food and directions to the nearest land from the U-boat. These small courtesies were part of a German plan to win sympathy for their side of the

war, especially from large neutral nations like the United States, which stayed out of the war until 1917.

As the war progressed keeping to the regulations became harder. In addition to submarine attacks the German navy sent out light cruisers to intercept and capture or destroy cargo ships bound for Great Britain. Before long the British Royal Navy sank most of these surface raiders, leaving only the U-boats to cut off Britain's supply lines. The ruler of Germany, Kaiser Wilhelm, had to make a choice: continue obeying the rules of engagement, which would take time and let ships slip into British ports, or attack all ships around the British Isles without warning. Wilhelm, on the advice of the commander of the fleet, Admiral Alfred von Tirpitz, approved the blockade. On February 5, 1915, the German government announced that its U-boats no longer would obey the rules of engagement and that after February 18 any ship

Germany's Kaiser Wilhelm declared in 1915 that U-boats would no longer adhere to the rules of engagement followed by other warships.

The German U-20, made famous by its attack on the passenger liner Lusitania. *The sinking of the* Lusitania *claimed hundreds of lives and created an international outcry.*

found in British waters would be torpedoed. Even ships flying under neutral flags, such as that of the United States, were at risk, the Germans warned.

From March 28 to May 7, 1915, U-boats sank three ships: an American cargo ship, the *Gulflight*, and the British passenger liners *Falaba* and *Lusitania*. Of the three events, the sinking of the *Lusitania* by the U-20, under the command of Walther Schweiger, created the greatest international outcry. Nearly 2,000 people died, among them 139 American passengers. While German newspapers celebrated the sinking as a success of German warfare, America and the neutral nations of Europe condemned the attack as an act of barbarity.

American anger was heightened by the sinking of the *Gulflight*, which had been torpedoed just six days before the attack on the *Lusitania*. Kaiser Wilhelm himself soured toward his U-boat force. The last thing he wished to do was anger the still-neutral Americans into declaring war against his country. After the sinking of the *Lusitania*, the Kaiser ordered his submarine captains to hold

their fire if they were not certain that their target was a British ship.

For the next year and a half U-boats concentrated on more strategic meth-

The Lusitania, *in New York Harbor in 1907. America and the neutral nations of Europe viewed the German U-20 attack on the* Lusitania *as an act of barbarity.*

ods of interrupting sea trade to Britain. In August 1916 the U-53 made a trip across the Atlantic to sink British and other allied merchant ships outside America's territorial waters. This was an unfortunate decision on Germany's part, because the attacks renewed the American public's anger at Germany's wartime behavior.

Developments During Wartime

As the war progressed, U-boats became Germany's sole means of attacking any sort of ship, merchant ships as well as warships. German shipyards were converted into submarine factories. From mid-1916 to the end of the war, 845 U-boats were launched and saw service in the Atlantic, the North Sea, and the Mediterranean Sea.

British, and later American, warships fought back as best they could, mixing old styles of combat—such as ramming subs on the surface—with new devices that could attack submarines as they hid beneath the waves. These devices were depth charges, can-shaped bombs that were tossed overboard from destroyers and other surface ships. Pressure triggers set off these bombs, nicknamed ash cans, when they reached the depth where the submarine was likely to be hiding. The attacking ships would drop a number of depth charges in a pattern around an area where the sub might be. If the pattern was thorough, or the ship lucky, one or more ash cans would blow up right next to the sub, ripping it open

Ready for war, German U-boats line a dock in 1914. The German government immediately recognized the advantages of being able to carry out a silent and sudden attack. As a result, Germany assembled a more advanced submarine fleet than any other nation.

The American L-4 was sent to the British Isles to support British forces in 1917. Because its crew was inexperienced and unprepared for combat, the L-4's mission failed.

for the sea to enter, sinking the boat and drowning its crew.

The British developed a number of other practices that offered a fair amount of protection from U-boat attack. Groups of destroyers escorted convoys of merchant ships across the Atlantic, increasing the chance that a submarine would be spotted before it could attack. If a U-boat did manage to sink a ship, the destroyers were able to attack and sink the submarine before it could get away and attack other ships. Great Britain also formed a fleet of decoys, merchant vessels that appeared to be unarmed but really were equipped with hidden guns and other weapons. These vessels, called Q-ships, were responsible for sinking a handful of U-boats by the war's end.

Although Great Britain's traditional surface fleets carried out most of the navy's missions, British submarines were not idle during the war. Besides claiming the war's first kill, British submarines wreaked havoc among German and Turkish ships in the Sea of Marmara, a body of water between the Mediterranean and Black seas. The British submarine E11 alone sank more than one hundred enemy ships in this area, despite being bombed by a Turkish seaplane and playing a form of underwater tag with the UB-14, a small German U-boat that was hauled overland specifically to stop the British submarine attacks.

The American submarine fleet, on the other hand, was not ready for combat by the time the United States entered the war in April 1917. Twelve U.S. submarines were sent to support British operations in the Azores and around the British Isles. But the only action the sub crews engaged in were attacks by American and British warships that mistook them for the enemy.

Two American submarines, the L-4 and the L-11, had a chance to sink U-boats off the coast of Ireland but failed. The L-4 came near two U-boats at different times, but each time missed its target completely. The L-11 sent two torpedoes straight and true toward a U-boat, but the second torpedo ran faster toward the target than the first one. As

A remarkable 1918 photograph captures a torpedoed ship in the moments before it sinks into its watery grave. A crew member can be seen dangling from a rope (top) as the last lifeboat pulls away.

the sub's captain watched through his periscope, the second torpedo caught up with the first, hit it, and blew itself and its mate up.

The Impact of the U-boats

Although, in the end, Germany lost World War I, Germany's U-boats dominated the underwater realm. Despite the convoys, the Q-ships, and the depth charge dropping destroyers, these submarines nearly defeated Britain's attempts to keep its supply lines open. By the time America entered the war in 1917, food and other goods were severely rationed in Britain. Some historians suggest that, if the war had not ended in 1918, Britain would have had to surrender to keep from starving.

The U-boats of World War I destroyed the idea that combat at sea could be conducted according to the old rules of courtesy. In order for submarines to be effective, they had to approach their targets silently and strike suddenly. Under the new rules of naval combat all seagoing vessels—whether merchant ship or warship—risked attack during wartime.

German and British submarines also created a whole new area of threat for warships. In the future lookouts would not have the luxury of simply watching the horizon for enemy warships. They now had to scan the waves for enemy periscopes and listen through underwater microphones for the sounds of enemy propellers or, worse, enemy torpedoes.

Wartime Workhorses

During World War I submarines were technological wonders that were regarded with suspicion by the world's naval powers. Aside from Germany's U-boats submarines were rarely used as major ships of war, but rather as undercover raiders in tightly controlled enemy waters. During World War II submarines became front line workhorses in the battle to keep enemy nations from moving and supplying their troops. While they still raided ships of commerce, they also became more aggressive in action against surface warships.

Submarines Between the Wars

In general the world's navies shrank soon after World War I. Most political leaders around the globe believed the world would never again experience war on so broad a scale as the war that had just ended. To them, it made no sense to spend money maintaining large war fleets. Moreover, no civilized nation wanted to seem aggressive in the new climate of world peace.

During the Washington armament conference of 1921 and 1922, the major powers tried to set and enforce limits on the size of each country's land and sea forces. But these limits were enforced selectively and temporarily. Many nations later went back on their agreements, strengthening their forces at the same time that potential foes were weakening theirs. And in those nations that were committed to honoring their agreements, military leaders knew the idea of long-lasting world peace was a fantasy and pushed for whatever improvements in land and naval forces they could get from their governments.

As part of its surrender terms Germany was banned from building any U-boats and all but a few types of surface warships. In 1922 America, Great Britain, France, Italy, and Japan signed an agreement limiting the size and number of ships in their navies. Great Britain lobbied for a ban on all military submarines, but its delegates tried to

A German U-boat remains undetected after attacking nearby ships. Arms treaties after World War I prohibited Germany from building more of these deadly subs.

PERISCOPES

The great disadvantage of early submarines was that the pilot had to come to the surface to gain a view of the surrounding waters. Once above the surface, the submarine could be seen and attacked. As Simon Lake, the builder of the *Argonaut* put it, "Cruising on the surface with the conning tower exposed would only be a target in wartime. I want to get my seeing eye above the surface in something so small that it will not attract attention." Lake's solution to this problem was the periscope, a long tube that conducts light from the surface to the submarine below.

In a simple periscope entering light is reflected downward by a prism. The light passes through a series of lenses that magnify the image and keep the light rays from spreading out and being absorbed by the walls of the tube. At the bottom of the tube, a second prism directs the light toward the eyepiece. A final lens focuses the light so that it forms a clear image in the eyepiece.

Most modern submarines have at least two periscopes, one large and one small. The large periscope provides exploratory views of enemy territory and can be used at night. The smaller, slimmer periscope is harder to detect and so is usually reserved for use before or during attacks.

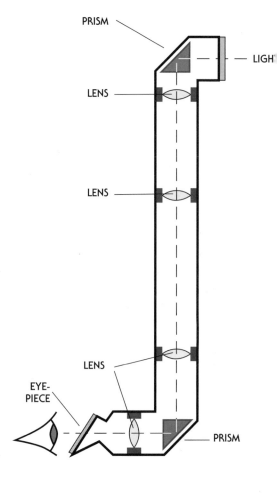

prove their case by using long-winded technical reasons to explain why submarines were not effective weapons. The other delegates quickly grew bored with the British debate—which did not explain why supposedly unsound submarines had nearly caused the economic destruction of the island kingdom—and virtually ignored the question of submarines altogether. The only limits the resulting arms treaty imposed were on the number of submarines each nation could build.

With few restrictions on submarine construction, aside from the ban on Germany, some nations began making

A Japanese I-boat prepares for its journey at sea. Built in the 1930s to expand Japan's navy, these large and well-armed submarines were capable of patrolling the western Pacific for weeks at a time.

bigger, more powerful, and better-armed submarines. The years between 1921 and 1938 saw a small explosion in submarine design. France had one of the most progressive, and certainly one of the most popular, submarines of this time: the *Surcouf*, which featured two forward-pointing eight-inch guns, two smaller deck guns, eighty torpedoes, and a small seaplane that was carried behind the conning tower and was used to spot targets. A series of smaller French subs, the Redoubtable class, or series, had torpedo tubes mounted on pivots in the conning tower in addition to four tubes at the bow. The pivoting tubes were designed to launch torpedoes toward nearly any nearby target

while the subs were on the surface. The *Surcouf*'s weapons performed well, and the sub fought against the Germans in World War II as far west as the Gulf of Mexico. However, the Redoubtables never were able to get their torpedoes to run accurately, except when they were fired from one of the bow tubes.

Expansion

The Japanese and Americans also continued developing their submarine technology. Japanese leaders in the 1930s wanted to expand Japan's political and military presence in their region. Toward this end Japan's warship and submarine construction program grew. The Japanese navy began ordering large, well-armed submarines. American politicians and military leaders, concerned about Japanese intentions, called for development of long-range subs capable of traveling thousands of miles.

The submarines built by both Japan and the United States were almost identical in size and performance. They were able to travel between ten thousand and fifteen thousand nautical miles on a single patrol without having to refuel. The size of the Pacific Ocean demanded submarines that were capable of these long-range journeys. Japan wanted its submarines, which were called I-boats, to be able to cruise along the northern rim of the Pacific and patrol the west coast of America for weeks without support. America needed subs that could make extended patrols in the western Pacific from their bases in Pearl Harbor and the Philippines.

The Rebirth of the U-Boat

The ban against German submarine building was as much a failure as was the attempt to eliminate war by reducing the world's navies. Although the U-boats of World War I had been destroyed or sent to Great Britain and America for study, the people who built and sailed them were still alive. Many of these people felt that Germany would one day return to its status as a world power but that this would be achieved only by keeping its submarine program alive. Working together they discovered a way around the ban on German sub building. German companies had been forbidden from building submarines in

Gustav Krupp found a way around the post-World War I ban on submarine building and kept Germany's submarine program alive.

Germany for the German navy. But there was no law banning German engineers from designing and building submarines outside Germany.

Gustav Krupp, whose company had built Germany's first Simon Lake submarine, sent forty employees to a firm his company owned in the Netherlands. The engineers designed new generations of U-boats, as well as the equipment and methods needed to build them. Krupp's company then sold the blueprints and construction guidelines to nations that, for the most part, had been friendly to German interests: Japan, Turkey, Spain, Finland, and the Netherlands.

Once these nations set up their own U-boat factories, Krupp began secretly buying U-boat parts and stockpiling them in Germany. In 1932, Adolf

Dozens of German submarines await deployment during World War II. Karl Dönitz (below) played a large part in the rebuilding of Germany's submarine fleet.

Hitler's Nazi party gained control of the German government. Hitler established himself as dictator in 1934. One of his first acts as dictator was to renounce the bans on German rearmament and to begin rebuilding the German military. Secret submarine yards were built along Germany's North Sea coast. Soon the stockpiles of U-boat parts were assembled into functional U-boats, and the submarine factories in Europe and Japan soon were contributing to the rearming of Germany.

Planning for War

Of the World War I U-boat sailors who had survived the war, an officer named Karl Dönitz was the most active in rebuilding Germany's sub fleet. At the end of the war, Dönitz had transferred to what remained of Germany's surface navy, where he eventually became captain of a cruiser. He also kept in touch with submarine designers in the Netherlands throughout the 1920s and 1930s. Meanwhile, he established a covert, or undercover, program in Germany to train the crews who would staff these subs in the next war. Though training submarine crews was officially forbidden, training crews to hunt submarines was not.

Dönitz set up an antisubmarine warfare school in Germany that exploited this legal loophole. "How can sailors fight submarines if they do not know how submarines operate?" Dönitz replied when outsiders asked why some officers and enlisted men were being taught the theories and techniques of U-boat operations. Officially, these men were preparing to protect Germany against submarine attacks in future conflicts. In reality, they were being shaped into the most elite fighting force in the German military.

Dönitz was equally evasive with his Nazi superiors in the German government. The rest of Germany's armed forces were forced to include party-trained political officers, who spread Nazi propaganda and politics among the troops. This tactic was part of Hitler's plan to brainwash the nation into accepting him not only as the leader of Germany, but also as its savior. Dönitz, however, refused to allow the Nazis to meddle with the training of his submarine crews.

Dönitz told Nazi party officials that mixing in politics would distract the new sub force from its training and would lead to an inefficient U-boat fleet. The real reason for the exclusion was that Dönitz wanted his crews' loyalty focused on Germany first and—as he did not want Hitler to have greater control over the submarine fleet than did its commander—on himself second.

As his sub crews were training for Hitler's coming war of German expansion, Dönitz was developing a technique that would give his U-boats an even greater war record than the U-boats of the last war had achieved. He knew

Adolf Hitler addresses his troops at a 1933 rally. Hitler later renounced the ban on rearmament imposed on his country after World War I and began rebuilding the German military.

An allied tanker is swallowed by the sea after being torpedoed by a German submarine in 1942. German U-boat crews were well-trained and prepared for warfare. The U-boats had a devastating effect on World War II Allied forces.

that, once war broke out, the British would fall back on the merchant convoy system that had effectively countered Germany's submarines during World War I. The success of the convoy, Dönitz realized, was that it had only had to deal with one or two U-boats at a time. If a group of submarines attacked a convoy, he thought, the results would be different. Some of the subs could distract the escorting warships while one or two others could sink some, if not all, of the merchant ships.

As he began working out the details of how these sub groups would operate,

Dönitz saw that they would be attacking convoys much like a pack of wolves attacks a herd of cows or elk. Thus, these small task forces of U-boats became known as wolf packs.

From Hunters to Hunted

When World War II began in 1939, Germany's U-boats were ready. The U-boats had a devastating effect on Britain's seaborne supply lines and, indeed, on the entire Allied war effort. Individual U-boats and wolf packs appeared to come out of nowhere and vanish into nowhere, leaving only sinking ships and castaway crews as evidence of their presence. They were similar in design to their World War I couterparts—weapons that could sail rather than ships that had weapons. And, like their predecessors, the crews had to make do with what little space was not taken up by machinery.

Attempts to stick to the time-honored rules of engagement again proved only that submarines could not operate under those rules. In fact the first submarine attack of World War II, made on the day Germany declared war against Great Britain, directly violated those rules. Mistaking the British cruise liner *Athenia* for a troopship, the captain of the U-30 sank her with two torpedoes, killing 118 passengers, 22 of whom were citizens of the still-neutral United States. The attack angered the British, who saw it as a repeat of the sinking of the *Lusitania*. The attack also angered Hitler, who had wanted the war to be seen by ordinary citizens around the world as Germany's attempt to regain power and prestige stolen from it at the end of World War I. The sinking of the *Athenia*, Hitler knew, could shatter this image. All German records of the attack were destroyed, and Germany's propaganda experts attempted to shift the blame for the attack to the British Royal Navy. The German government claimed that Prime Minister Winston Churchill had ordered the ship sunk to whip up public hatred of Germany and to gain the sympathy of neutral nations.

To regain Hitler's trust in the U-boats, Dönitz planned an attack on the British naval base at Scapa Flow, a harbor on Scotland's North Sea coast. The Scapa Flow supposedly was one of the

To protect Hitler's image, the Nazis blamed Prime Minister Winston Churchill of Britain for the German attack on a British cruise liner.

best-defended of the British bases, with floating barriers and sunken ships blocking the entrances against submarine entry. Yet one U-boat, the U-47, managed to slip through these defenses on October 14, 1939, and sink the flagship of the British North Seas Fleet without being detected. This victory marked the start of a five-year campaign in which Germany's U-boats devastated Allied shipping on both sides of the Atlantic.

Japan had similar successes in the Pacific in 1942, the year of America's entry into World War II. During that time, Japanese submarines sank dozens of U.S. warships, including the aircraft carriers USS *Yorktown* and USS *Wasp*.

American sub crews were unprepared for the reality of submarine warfare. The American government in the 1930s did not believe that Japan would

A Japanese submarine captured by U.S. forces after the disastrous 1941 Pearl Harbor attack. The U.S. submarine fleet suffered at first from inexperienced crews and poorly designed torpedoes. Improvements in both areas led to later Allied victories on the Atlantic and Pacific fronts.

dare attack such a large military and industrial power as the United States. Navy officials in particular believed that, even if Japan did declare war, the U.S. surface and submarine fleets could easily defeat any Japanese warships they came across. This lax attitude crossed over into the training that American armed forces, and especially the submarine fleet, received through 1941.

Disaster and Recovery

On December 7, 1941, carrier-based Japanese aircraft attacked Pearl Harbor, the U.S. Navy's base in Hawaii. Within two days the American submarine fleet found itself trying to locate and sink enemy ships. Most submarine commanders had been trained during the twenty-three peaceful years after World War I and were not able to make the type of aggressive attacks needed in wartime. They had been trained to listen for enemy ships' propellers while submerged deep underwater, rather than cruising on the surface or scanning through their periscopes. They

also had been trained to make cautious, careful attack runs that supposedly would keep their subs from being detected until after they had attacked. In reality, these methods allowed most sub-

Most American submarine commanders were not trained to use their periscopes to scan for enemy ships. They relied on the sound of ship propellers for locating targets.

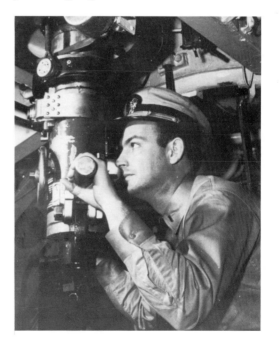

SONAR

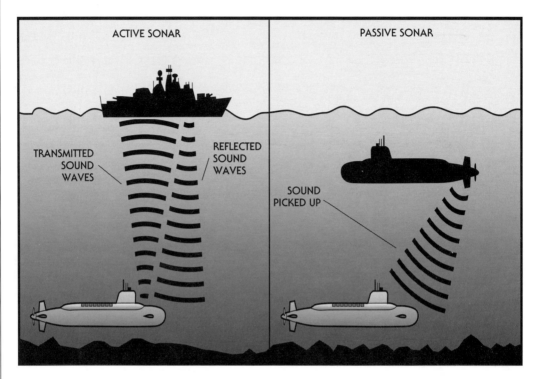

ACTIVE SONAR

TRANSMITTED SOUND WAVES

REFLECTED SOUND WAVES

PASSIVE SONAR

SOUND PICKED UP

The word sonar is short for so(und) na(vigation) and r(anging). As the name suggests, sonar uses sound to navigate underwater. There are two kinds of sonar: active and passive.

An active sonar device emits a sound underwater. The sound travels or is transmitted in waves. The transmitted sound waves travel through the water until they strike a distant object, such as an enemy ship. The sound waves are reflected, or bounced off, the object back toward the submarine. The submarine's underwater microphone picks up these sound wave echoes. By measuring the time it takes for the echoes to return, the submarine's sonar equipment can tell the user how far away the object is, how large it is, and whether or not it is moving.

Because an active sonar system measures echoes, it is sometimes called an echosounder.

The problem with active sonar is that enemy ships equipped with underwater microphones can also pick up the sound waves and use them to locate the submarine that is transmitting them. Passive sonar avoids this problem by not transmitting sound waves at all. With passive sonar, underwater microphones pick up sound waves naturally given off by the motion of a submarine. Computers are used to help the sonar operator tell the difference between natural ocean sounds, such as those made by whales, and the sounds made by enemy submarines and ships.

The damaged USS Yorktown *attacked by a Japanese submarine during the Battle of Midway, slowly sinks. Japanese submarines sank dozens of U.S. warships.*

marines' targets either to escape or to attack their attackers.

The submarine fleet had another problem to deal with. Until 1943 the torpedoes they used were unable to sink most of their targets. Either the torpedoes ran too deep and passed under the hulls of enemy ships, or they struck without exploding. Officials both in the navy and in the government's Bureau of Ordnance, which had designed the torpedoes, refused to admit that anything was wrong. They usually cited human error as the problem.

Eventually the torpedo problems were corrected, but only after Charles Lockwood, an American vice admiral who commanded the Pacific submarine fleet, took charge. Tests revealed flaws in the torpedo depth gauges and detonators. The gauges were miscalculating torpedo depths by up to eleven feet,

and the detonators were breaking before they could set off the warheads. Redesign began immediately. Within a short time the problems had been solved.

The year 1943 marked the beginning of greater Allied victories on the Atlantic and Pacific fronts. After attacking and boarding a U-boat, the crew of a British destroyer captured the secret codes Admiral Dönitz used to command his U-boat fleet. British and American warships used this information to locate and sink German subs. The U-boat fleet still managed to attack Allied warships, troop transports, and cargo ships, but with less frequency than before.

In the Pacific Ocean, on the other hand, the American submarine fleet gained the upper hand over the Japanese navy by sheer hard work. De-

American troops on the deck of a docked submarine greet the USS Tinosa as it returns to Pearl Harbor after patrolling Japanese waters in 1945. The end of World War II signaled the end of extensive submarine warfare.

spite the plague of malfunctioning torpedoes, American subs sank dozens of Japanese merchant and military supply ships each month. This loss was so great that the Japanese government began using its I-boats to deliver much needed supplies to its troops that were scattered throughout the islands of the South Pacific. Before long nearly all Japanese submarines were being used to carry cargo, and American ships were crossing the Pacific almost without fear of attack. Once the U.S. submarine fleet received the redesigned torpedoes, even more Japanese merchant and war ships were sent to the bottom.

The Last Submarine War

By the end of World War II submarines had been proven to be effective weapons of war. As in World War I, Germany's U-boats had nearly starved the British Isles. In the Pacific the American submarine fleet kept Japanese troops from receiving weapons and supplies, helping to force them to retreat from captured islands. But World War II was the last time submarines were used in an all-out campaign against enemy shipping. None of the conflicts after 1945 required the type of fighting that submarines were designed for. In the Korean War of the early 1950s, the USS *Perch*, a World War II-vintage submarine, was used to land a small company of British commandos for a night raid. In the Vietnam War of the 1960s and 1970s, there was no need for submarines at all. Instead, submarines were to have an even more vital role to play in keeping an even greater war than World War II from breaking out.

CHAPTER 5

Weapons of Deterrence

The end of World War II in 1945 sparked another series of military cutbacks around the world. In the United States bureaucrats and navy admirals were convinced that air power was the key to future naval battles. Although the submarine service had struck a major blow against Japanese supply ships, it was the navy carrier forces that kept the Japanese navy at bay. In the battle of Midway in the central Pacific and the battle of the Coral Sea in the South Pacific, in particular, navy fighters, bombers, and torpedo planes did the actual fighting. In the future, the experts said, naval aviation would replace the big guns of past naval battles. The only need for ships like destroyers and cruisers would be to support beach landings and to protect carriers from enemy airplanes and submarines.

This idea of the navy as a carrier-dominated force left little room for submarines. Military experts figured they would be used for fleet defense, for raids on merchant ships, and for spying on enemy fleets. They doubted, however, that there would be a major role for submarines in future conflicts. But within ten years after the end of World War II, a dynamic naval officer forced a series of design changes that turned submarines from weapons of warfare into weapons of deterrence.

Captain Hyman Rickover foresaw the potential of a nuclear-powered naval fleet as a deterrent against future warfare.

The Development of the Nuclear Navy

In 1946 Captain Hyman Rickover was in charge of mothballing the navy's unneeded warships—stripping them of most of their equipment and anchoring them in storage berths. This process was a nightmare of organization, discipline, and attention to detail. It required the movement of hundreds of ships, thousands of sailors, and an avalanche of parts and paperwork. It was exactly the

Rickover demonstrates how a nuclear reactor gives submarines and warships greater power and speed. The U.S. government was not eager to adopt nuclear power for submarines.

type of task Rickover loved.

A skilled electrical engineer, Rickover had earned a reputation as a strict perfectionist who could complete any task assigned to him. During World War II he was placed in charge of the electrical section of the Bureau of Ships, which oversaw all U.S. Navy ship construction. In his first few months he redesigned the section's inefficient catalog and distribution system, which had delayed many ships and construction yards from receiving needed electrical parts. He also examined many electrical parts and redesigned those he thought were poorly made. He then forced manufacturers to either rebuild the components according to his design or risk losing their government contracts. (His run-ins with the manufacturers and

with his superior officers about these requirements gave him another reputation—that of a man with no regard for the egos of those he thought lazy, stupid, or incompetent.)

As Rickover was supervising the partial dismantling of the navy, another job came along that was even better suited to his abilities. A group of army and navy officers was being sent to the government's atomic energy research center at Oak Ridge, Tennessee. Their mission was to determine possible military uses for atomic energy other than nuclear weapons. Rickover, a proven expert in naval electrical engineering, was transferred to this group.

While at Oak Ridge, Rickover was able to study a small working nuclear reactor that provided power to the research complex. After learning how the reactor worked, Rickover became convinced that similar devices should be used to power navy ships. Ships powered by nuclear reactors, he reasoned, would be able to go longer without refueling than they could using conventional diesel engines. Because nuclear power promised huge amounts of energy from fuel cells as small as a golf ball, nuclear-powered ships should be able to go faster than conventional ships, as well.

Rickover was especially eager to design such a nuclear-powered propulsion system for submarines. Steam generated by a sub's nuclear reactor could be used to power the electric motors that run the sub on the surface and underwater. Since a nuclear reactor does not use any oxygen, a nuclear-powered submarine would be able to cruise without surfacing at all, except to bring on fresh supplies of food or to give crews a chance to relax on shore. Any oxygen the crew needed could be processed from seawater. As in diesel-electric subs, carbon dioxide would be removed from the air by special chemical filters.

Rickover realized that nuclear power could lead to the creation of a submarine that spends all its time underwater, limited only by the crew's endurance. (Technically, even the submarines of the two world wars, which had to surface to recharge their batteries and replenish their air, were submersible surface ships, not true submarines.) Rickover gathered support for his plan from the other members of the task force, as well as from some of the Oak Ridge scientists, who began designing a submarine reactor in their spare time.

Officials at the Bureau of Ships did not share Rickover's conviction that nuclear power would be a boon for the navy. Atomic energy was too new and untested to risk using in submarines, which were dangerous enough, they said. And building a nuclear-powered submarine would simply cost too much, no matter what benefits might be gained. When the task force recommended that the bureau look into adapting nuclear power for naval use, the bureau dismissed the idea. Rickover was furious when he heard the news. He *knew* that the navy should adapt nuclear power for use on warships and submarines and felt that the bureaucrats at the Bureau of Ships were merely hiding from a technology they did not understand. For the next four years Rickover pushed his idea of a nuclear navy to members of Congress, top navy officials, and anyone else who could help him win his case.

"Nautilus Ninety North"

As the years went by, Rickover gained support from politically powerful figures both in the navy and in Congress. Finally, in 1952, Congress approved a plan to build a nuclear-powered submarine. Rickover was put in charge of the navy's nuclear program, both as head of the Bureau of Ships nuclear reactors branch and as head of the Atomic Energy Commission's naval reactors branch. This double authority allowed Rickover to bring his exacting standards to bear on the construction of the first nuclear-powered submarine, the USS *Nautilus.*

The company that won the contract was the Electric Boat Company, the same submarine construction firm that

The world's first nuclear submarine, the USS Nautilus, *set records for speed and endurance, overcoming misgivings about the benefits of a nuclear-powered submarine.*

John Holland started in the late 1890s. Although Holland's first government project suffered from an incompetent government design committee, the Electric Boat Company's newest government contract pushed it toward higher standards than it had ever reached before.

Rickover demanded that every part on board the *Nautilus* meet with his approval. He tested equipment designed especially for the atomic submarine by placing it on board old World War II subs. With these tests he determined whether the equipment could stand up to the intense pressure and rugged conditions the *Nautilus* would face. Rickover chastised engineers whose designs failed these tests.

The USS *Nautilus* was ready for service in 1954. It looked a little like the surface-cruising submarines of World War II. The sub had a wedge-shaped hull with a blunt bow that made it resemble a sperm whale. Submarine designers thought this shape was the most efficient design for pushing through the water while submerged or on the surface. The *Nautilus* was also designed for stable surface cruising in case the

nuclear generator failed. Nobody really knew if the world's first nuclear submarine would work.

Any misgivings proved groundless from the first day the *Nautilus* took to the water in Groton, Connecticut. The

The Nautilus *is launched into the Thames River in Connecticut for its initial surface trial.*

One of the biggest advantages of nuclear-powered subs was their ability to stay submerged for long periods of time. The USS Seawolf *set a record by staying underwater for sixty days, a duration that is common for modern submarines.*

nuclear power plant drove the submarine underwater at nineteen knots, or roughly twenty-two miles an hour. For a submarine to travel this fast underwater was a major achievement. Conventionally powered submarines could go this fast only while using their diesel engines on the surface. As Rickover had figured, the *Nautilus* also was capable of cruising underwater as long as the crew's supplies held out. On one cruise the crew stayed underwater for more than eleven days. This feat must have seemed remarkable to old-time submarine sailors, for whom ten hours underwater was a dangerously long dive.

The *Nautilus* went on to set other records. Perhaps its most impressive accomplishment was sailing from the Pacific Ocean to the Atlantic under the Arctic ice cap in August 1958. This journey was a much publicized event, and the entire nation was electrified when it heard news of the message sent out by the submarine's captain, Commander William Anderson: "Nautilus Ninety North." At 11:15 P.M. on August 3 the *Nautilus* had crossed earth's geographic north pole, proving both that a passage between the Pacific and Atlantic oceans existed and that a submarine could make use of this new shortcut.

Two more atomic submarines were built along the lines of the *Nautilus*—the USS *Seawolf*, launched in 1956, and the USS *Skate*, launched in 1957. In August 1958, three days after the *Nautilus* passed under the North Pole, the *Skate* surfaced in an opening in the Arctic ice pack about forty miles from the North Pole. Navy officials—Rickover included—felt that it was vital for submarines sailing under the ice pack to be able to break through to receive or transmit messages. Seven months later the *Skate* set another record by breaking

THE NUCLEAR POWERED SUBMARINE

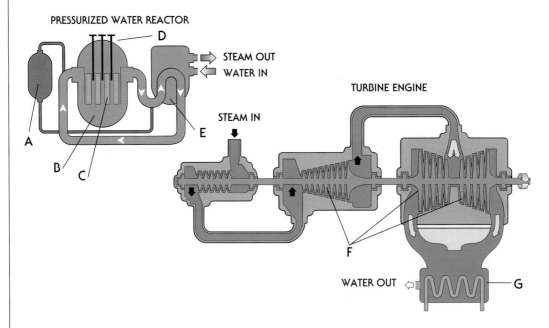

PRESSURIZED WATER REACTOR

D

STEAM OUT
WATER IN

TURBINE ENGINE

STEAM IN

A

B
C

E

F

WATER OUT

G

The engines of many modern submarines are powered by the energy released when atoms split apart. This energy is known as nuclear power.

The splitting of the atoms takes place in a pressurized water reactor. This process begins when a high pressure stream of water passes from the pressurizer (A) into the reactor core (B). Inside the reactor core are fuel rods (C) containing uranium atoms. When the atoms split, causing a reaction known as nuclear fission, a great deal of heat is generated. Control rods (D) inserted into the fuel rods help slow the reaction down. This allows the water to be heated to about 570 degrees Fahrenheit.

This superheated water never leaves the reactor. On its way back to the reactor core, however, it passes through the heat exchanger (E), which contains cool water. As the superheated water passes through

the heat exchanger, the cool water warms and turns to high-pressure steam. The steam passes into a turbine engine.

Inside the turbine engine the steam passes through a series of blades. The blades (F) are connected to a drive shaft. As the steam progresses to each set of blades, the blades turn. The turning blades rotate the drive shaft. The drive shaft transmits the engine's revolutions to the propeller, causing the propeller to turn.

At the same time, the steam is channeled into a condenser (G), where it cools. The cooled steam becomes water and the water returns to the heat exchanger where it begins the cycle again.

In this way, nuclear energy and steam drive the submarine's propeller. Steam from the reactor also generates all of the submarine's electricity.

through the ice pack to surface at the North Pole.

These successes not only proved the worth of naval nuclear power, but they also revitalized Hyman Rickover's navy career. During his battles to build the *Nautilus*, Rickover had twice been passed over for promotion to rear admiral. Normally, an officer who is passed over twice either retires or is discharged from the navy. But Rickover stayed in the service to see his task through. His determination won him widespread respect both in the navy and in the government, a respect that was increased with the success of the *Nautilus* and the other submarines. He was eventually promoted to admiral, the navy's highest rank, and was allowed to stay in the navy until he was eighty-two, far beyond the normal retirement age. Because of his work with nuclear submarines, and with other nuclear-powered navy ships, Rickover is referred to by military historians as the founder of the nuclear navy.

New Designs, New Duties

After these first three atomic submarines were launched, the navy's sub designers realized there was no need to keep on using the old pointed-bow outer hulls that made surface travel easier. The three submarines had proved that their nuclear power systems were reliable and that sailors could live and work while submerged for weeks at a time. While the outer hull was still a necessity, it could now be given a more streamlined shape, identical to the hulls of John Holland's and Simon Lake's early submarines. Tests starting in 1953 with a diesel-electric submarine, the USS *Albacore*, showed that a fat, sausage-shaped outer hull—much like the one John Holland used for the *Fenian Ram*—could give submarines an underwater speed of twenty-five knots, nearly twenty-nine miles an hour, or more.

The first nuclear submarine built with this new type of outer hull, the USS *Skipjack*, was launched in 1958. If war broke out, its mission was to attack enemy surface ships or submarines, just as earlier submarines had done.

Two years later, however, the philosophy of submarine warfare changed dramatically. Engineers in the United States and the Soviet Union created rockets that could carry nuclear bombs thousands of miles across oceans or continents in a few minutes. These ballistic missiles, and later intercontinental ballistic missiles, marked a new level of

The outer hull of the USS Skipjack *was more streamlined than previous nuclear-powered vessels. Its shape allowed it to reach a speed of twenty-five knots.*

tension in the cold war between America and the Soviet Union. Politicians and military experts in both nations knew that to keep the upper hand they would need a way to station these missiles near each other's borders. At the same time, these missiles would have to be hidden from the other side. Land-based missiles could never be kept a secret. High-flying spy planes and surveillance satellites would eventually find their underground storage places. A submerged missile-carrying submarine, though, would leave no trace of its presence on the surface of the ocean.

The Soviet Union was the first nation to put ballistic missiles on board a submarine. Called the Golf class by Western nations, these diesel-electric subs were launched in the mid-1950s and were in service by 1958. They carried three short-range missiles in vertical tubes that were mounted in an extended conning tower.

To counter the threat of these Golf class subs, the American navy developed a new type of underwater vessel—nuclear-powered ballistic missile sub-

marines, nicknamed "boomers." The first of these subs, the USS *George Washington*, was an attack sub that was altered to carry twelve missiles that could be launched underwater. The modifications themselves were simple. The sub's hull was chopped in half just behind the conning tower. Shipyard workers then installed a new section that contained twelve vertical launch tubes and their accompanying electronics and other hardware. This design turned the submarine into an underwater missile field, giving it thousands of times the destructive power of all the bombs dropped during World War II. The ballistic missiles themselves were loaded secretly later, after the submarine was launched.

This make-do approach worked well—the *George Washington* and other submarines of its class are still in service after more than thirty years of operation. Later generations of boomers were designed specifically as missile carriers.

The Soviet Union quickly followed America's lead into the realm of nuclear propulsion. The first Soviet nuclear-powered missile and attack subs were

The Soviet Golf class submarines were the first to carry ballistic missiles. These vessels completely changed the nature of submarine warfare.

To counter the threat of Soviet missile-carrying submarines, the United States developed and built a new class of submarines that included the USS George Washington. *This menacing sub carried twelve missiles that could be launched underwater.*

launched in 1958 and 1959. The presence of both American and Soviet boomers quickly led to an international policy of nuclear deterrence, or maintaining large quantities of nuclear weapons to discourage war. The threat of nuclear retaliation, especially from the nearly invisible missile-carrying subs, assured that neither country would be the first to launch a nuclear attack.

With the development of nuclear power, the U.S. Navy stopped ordering conventional submarines and gradually withdrew its diesel-electric boats from service. A few conventional subs were built for various experimental missions in the 1960s, and a few older subs were retained as targets and for similar duties. The government sold a number of other subs, some of which dated back to World War II, to friendly nations in South America and the Middle East. America committed itself to building the world's only all-nuclear submarine fleet. The Soviet Union decided it did not need the type of large, wide-ranging, and expensive submarine fleet that America was building. Instead, it built a mixed fleet, with nuclear-powered attack and missile subs for cruising across oceans and

A ballistic missile fired from a submarine shoots into the air and heads without warning toward its target.

diesel-electric submarines for patrols nearer to Soviet shores. Great Britain, France, and China—the only other nations to date to build and operate nuclear subs—also have a mix of nuclear and conventional submarines.

Submarine Warfare in Modern Times

For the last half of the twentieth century submarines have been used mainly as weapons of deterrence. Nuclear missile submarines go to sea with one primary mission: to hide and wait for an order to fire their missiles. For up to six months at a time the boomer crews are out of contact with the surface world, aside from brief messages transmitted from their families over radio bands re-

served for navy use. In case of a nuclear attack on the United States, these same radio bands would carry coded orders to these subs. Although the collapse of the Soviet Union has reduced the possibility of an all-out nuclear war, military experts have pointed out that many countries possess or are building nuclear weapons.

In fact, considering the hundreds of submarines that have been built since the end of World War II, it is remarkable how little they actually have been used in combat. Submarines have fired at hostile targets on only three occasions since the mid-1940s. In 1971 India and Pakistan were at war over the creation of an independent nation, Bangladesh, formerly East Pakistan. India supported the idea of the new nation and provided training to fighters from Bangladesh. Pakistan opposed the new nation, and attacked both the Bangladesh fighters and India. As part of the confrontation a Pakistani diesel-electric submarine, the *Hangor*, was sent out to harass Indian warships. Halfway through the war, which lasted two weeks, the *Hangor* came across two Indian frigates, or small warships, steaming out of the Gulf of Khambhat, north of Bombay, India. The *Hangor* fired torpedoes at the two targets, sinking one and damaging the other so badly it was forced to spend the rest of the short war in port.

Eleven years later Great Britain and the South American nation of Argentina were at war over the Falklands, a small group of islands off Argentina's southeast coast. Both nations claimed the Falklands as their territory, and in 1981 the Argentine army invaded the islands. As part of their operation to reclaim the islands, the British sent a task force of five submarines to patrol the

SUBMARINE WEAPONS

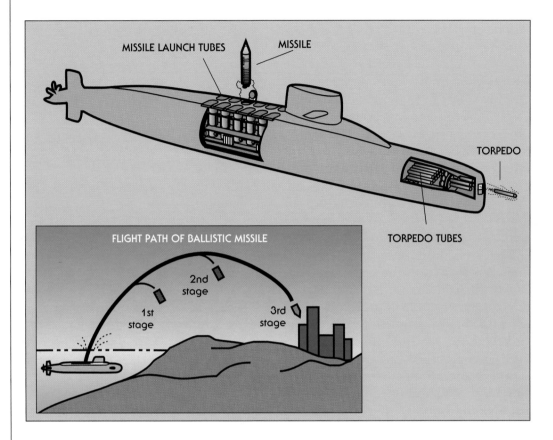

MISSILE LAUNCH TUBES

MISSILE

TORPEDO

TORPEDO TUBES

FLIGHT PATH OF BALLISTIC MISSILE

1st stage

2nd stage

3rd stage

Modern submarines, depending on their class, are equipped with one or more types of weapons. The three main types of weapons are torpedoes, cruise missiles, and submarine launched ballistic missiles (SLBM).

Torpedoes and cruise missiles are both launched from torpedo tubes located fore, aft, and amidships. Torpedoes are propeller-driven weapons that move through the water until they strike the hull of a ship or some other underwater target. Cruise missiles are launched underwater, but rise above the surface. Powered by a turbofan jet engine, the cruise missile flies above the surface of the water. Its electronic guiding system allows the missile to follow the contours of the sea and land on its way to its target. By flying close to the sea and land, cruise missiles avoid detection by radar systems.

Submarine launched ballistic missiles are fired from vertical tubes located amidships. The missiles are powered through the water by compressed gas and by three stages of rockets once they become airborne. Each rocket carries the missile a certain distance, then detaches and allows the next rocket to take over. The three rocket stages assure that the missile reaches its target, which can be thousands of miles away.

sea between the islands and the mainland. One of these submarines, the nuclear attack sub HMS *Conqueror,* sank the Argentine cruiser *General Belgrano* with two torpedoes.

The third submarine to fire on an enemy target since the 1940s was the USS *Louisville,* an American attack sub that took part in the Persian Gulf War of 1991. The war was an attempt to drive the army of Iraq out of Kuwait, a tiny, oil-rich nation that Iraq had invaded in August 1990. Although submarines primarily hunt other submarines and ships with torpedoes, in the 1970s the U.S. Navy had developed a cruise missile that could be fired from an attack or missile submarine's twenty-one-inch torpedo tubes. This missile, called the Tomahawk, became part of the regular weapon supply of nearly every attack sub in the fleet. Until the Gulf War the missile had never been used in combat. As part of Operation Desert Storm, the forty-three-day allied air and ground assault against Iraq, the *Louisville* and other attack submarines fired at and hit inland targets with these missiles.

The Tomahawk cruise missile, developed in the 1970s, was first employed during the Persian Gulf War in 1991.

A Changing Role in the Future

While these three attacks showed off the versatility of submarines, they also exposed the overriding limit on all submarine operations. Submarines are expensive to run and are most economically used in war when their primary mission is to destroy targets at sea. In most cases surface ships and aircraft carrying guided missiles can attack inland targets more effectively than can submarines.

The Future

The hundred years between the early 1890s and the early 1990s formed a kind of golden age of submarine development. From the time the first successful Holland and Lake boats entered service, submarines followed a path of almost constant improvement. Most of the submarines of the twentieth century have been built as warships. However, some subs have been built as research vessels. These craft let scientists explore the ocean depths and allow sub designers to study new methods of construction that make submarines even more at home in the sea.

The near future for submarines may be that they will be used as tools of research and recreational vehicles. By the 1980s nuclear and conventional, or nonnuclear, submarines contained some of the most advanced technology in the world. But the costs of building

Since their invention, submarines have improved consistently and dramatically. Although most submarines of the twentieth century were built as weapons of war, the future may see them used for other purposes including recreation and marine research.

The huge cost involved in building nuclear submarines has prompted government officials and the public to question the need for more of these expensive vessels.

and maintaining these vessels also grew. As the twentieth century draws to a close, government officials and the public alike are questioning the need to pay for these expensive warships.

Military Reductions

For nearly forty years the cold war between America and the Soviet Union fueled the fast growth of many navies' submarine fleets. In addition to the American and the Soviet navies, Great Britain, France, and China maintained fleets of nuclear attack subs and missile-carrying boomers. But the collapse of the Soviet Union in 1991, together with a series of recessions, has halted this type of energetic development.

Most nations having nuclear powered submarines either have canceled or have severely cut back on programs to develop new subs. Some nations have even stopped building some types of submarines altogether. Great Britain, for example, stopped building attack submarines in 1992, ninety-one years after John Holland supervised the construction of its first sub. And the ship-

yards that once built subs for the Soviet navy have stopped building nearly all submarines and surface ships.

A similar series of cutbacks has begun to take its toll on America's submarine fleets. One of the most dramatic of the effects is the drastic reduction in a series of advanced nuclear attack submarines that will have the largest weapons capacity in the world. These subs, the Seawolf class, also will be able to travel at a fairly high speed—twenty knots—without giving themselves away to other submarines or surface ships. Modern nuclear submarines can travel

Without the threat of war between the superpowers most nations have limited or stopped their production of nuclear submarines.

at speeds up to thirty-five knots. But subs traveling at such a high speed cannot help generating noise from their inner machinery, their propellers, and the flow of water over their hulls. Not only can sensitive underwater microphones pick up this noise, but the sub's own microphones and sonar are effectively deafened by the noise. The Seawolf class hulls are designed to muffle both interior and exterior noise.

Concern About Cost

Unfortunately, the cost of these and other innovations boosted the price to more than two billion dollars per submarine. Even so, advances in Soviet submarine design in anti-submarine warfare seemed to make quieter American submarines a necessity. Congress allowed the Navy to begin building the first three of a planned series of these super submarines. But by 1993 it was clear that the U.S. Navy had no need for a large force of these expensive warships. In September 1993 Secretary of Defense Les Aspin announced that the Navy planned to reduce its entire submarine fleet. Under this plan, the *Seawolf* and its two sister ships would be the only subs still under construction.

With the cost of increasingly advanced submarines no longer justified by the duties they will perform, the future of military submarines seems to be heading away from large fleets of giant subs. Over the next few decades the world's navies will focus on maintaining their older submarines and replacing outdated subs with vessels that are only slightly more advanced. America will hold on to its all-nuclear force of attack and missile submarines, although it will probably not spend a great deal of money to develop more advanced submarines. It also will maintain its position as the only nation in the world with such a submarine service. Many smaller nations have small submarine fleets made up of conventional boats built in English, Dutch, French, German, or Italian shipyards. These smaller navies plan to update their fleets, some of which have submarines that have been in service since the 1960s. Unless another war on the scale of World War II erupts, however, it is unlikely that the great sub fleets of the twentieth century will return.

Seeking Out the Pleasures of the Underwater World

While the world's navies have been slimming down their submarine fleets, the civilian world has begun to discover the pleasures of underwater travel. Starting in the mid-1980s a number of companies have offered hour-long underwater excursions in small, electric passenger submarines that take tourists along reefs and other scenic areas. These passenger submarines are technically a return to some of the subs of the 1880s and 1890s. They are powered by banks of electric batteries that can weigh a total of twenty thousand pounds or more. The subs are, of course, more advanced than their nineteenth-century counterparts, however. They can carry up to fifty passengers in pressurized, air-conditioned cabins, which are similar to those of small airplanes.

These subs, which are only about sixty-five feet long, have slow cruising speeds and narrow diving ranges. One hour at one and a half knots is the ex-

Tourist submarines (above and below) can take passengers up to 200 feet underwater to explore the wonders of sea life along reefs and scenic coastlines.

tent of their cruising radius, and their pressure hulls are designed to operate at a maximum depth of 150 to 200 feet. Despite being designed for only brief trips, each of these subs has a three-day reserve oxygen supply. Fortunately, since the first of these tourist subs started operations, none of them has had to use these emergency supplies.

Despite their expense—anywhere from $72 to $250 a trip—these rides are very popular. One tourist sub company, Atlantis Submarines International, reported taking more than 600,000 passengers on dives from 1986 to 1989. This company and others have been able to include in their operations many of the most popular tourism sites in the world. Their subs offer tours along reefs and coastlines in Hawaii, Guam, and Okinawa, Japan, and around the Caribbean islands of Grand Cayman, Barbados, and St. Thomas. Tourist subs may be the most profitable way to use submarines in commercial ventures. The few attempts at building submarine cargo carriers, such as the *Deutschland* (*Germany*) in World War I and the Japanese supply subs of World War II,

The Deutschland *was built to transport goods during World War I. The high costs and energy involved made the submarine a poor cargo carrier.*

showed that submarines do not make good merchant vessels. They use far more energy to transport goods than do traditional merchant ships.

Expedition to the North Pole

Possibly the greatest promise for submarines lies in their use as vessels of scientific exploration. One of the earliest and grandest attempts to adapt submarines for scientific use took place in 1931. Australian explorer Sir George Hubert Wilkins and Norwegian scientist Harald Sverdrup bought an obsolete American submarine, which they called *Nautilus,* for use in an expedition to the North Pole. The two explorers had a simple plan. Instead of risking a perilous journey across the ice pack, they would skim underneath it in a submarine fitted with a pair of skis on top of its hull. (The skis were designed by Simon Lake, who had started building submarines as research ships nearly forty years before.) They planned to submerge near the pole, travel a short way under the ice, and then raise the submarine until the skis pressed against the icy roof. This method was expected to allow the expedition to sail underwater to the pole in relative comfort, as if in an underwater sleigh.

The expedition planned to avoid the huge inverted, or upside down, mountains of ice that project downwards from the ice by keeping a constant watch through the sub's periscope. The sub was able to recharge its air and its batteries by surfacing in small areas of open water that sometimes form between blocks of Arctic ice. No one knows if Wilkins and Sverdrup planned to surface at the North Pole, though it is doubtful that the *Nautilus* could have broken through the heavy ice. Whatever their plans were, they were destined to fail for two reasons. First, the submarine became colder the farther north the expedition sailed. By the time the *Nautilus* reached the Arctic Ocean, frost and icicles were forming on the inside of the pressure hull. The members of the expedition and the submarine's crew had expected the drop in temperature and the accompanying discomfort. What they had not expected was the eerie wail that rang throughout the submarine as its skis dragged along under the ice. After only a few days of exposure to the hideous noise, the explorers decided to abandon the adventure.

The Arctic Circle

Although the *Nautilus* of 1931 never reached its goal, nuclear-powered subs from America and the Soviet Union did. On March 17, 1959, the American submarine USS *Skate* broke through the ice pack at the North Pole. (A year earlier, the *Skate* had surfaced in an open spot, or polynya, in the ice.) In 1959 the *Skate* proved that submarines could make their own openings, provided the ice was thin enough. This was a critical stage in the U.S. Navy's quest to use the Arctic Circle as a potential battleground. The ability to break through the ice meant that American missile subs could fire their weapons much closer to targets in the Northern Soviet Union. The same held true for Soviet submarines, however, which now had better access to sites in North America.

The *Skate*'s surfacing at the North Pole was just one event in a decades-long study of the Arctic Circle. Other submarines used their sonar to map the sea floor and find safe deep-water routes under the ice. They tracked the movement and formation of the ice pack so submarine captains would know what to expect at different times of the year. Some submarines even surfaced through the ice so their crews could send up weather balloons and study how the Arctic atmosphere behaved. These voyages were made mainly to gather data for wartime use. Nuclear

The USS Skate *parts the sea as it heads toward its destination, the icy waters of the North Pole.*

subs were ill equipped and too expensive for strictly scientific use.

Descent to the Deepest Place on Earth

For detailed underwater research scientists began building dozens of small submersible research craft capable of deep, short-term dives. Few of these vessels were submarines in a true sense. Instead, they were outgrowths of diving bells and bathyspheres, hollow metal balls lowered by cable from a surface ship that could carry a couple of scientists a few thousand feet deep.

One of the most famous of the early submersibles was the *Trieste*, built in the early 1950s by Swiss scientist Auguste Piccard. This submersible, called a bathyscaphe, carried scientists in a small metal sphere powered by electric batteries. A tank of gasoline above the sphere was used to float the craft back to the surface. This could be accomplished since gasoline is lighter than water and can withstand the pressure of steep ascents. For ballast the craft carried metal weights it dropped to return to the surface.

Though somewhat primitive, this craft was versatile and durable. In 1960 Piccard's son Jacques and U.S. Navy lieutenant Donald Walsh took the *Trieste* to the deepest place on earth: the Challenger Deep. The Challenger Deep is located in the Marianas Trench, two hundred miles south of Guam in the western Pacific. The *Trieste* dove more than six miles beneath the water's surface to reach the bottom of the Challenger Deep. Once reaching bottom,

The Trieste *and its crew made a dive that took them more than six miles below the water's surface to the deepest place on earth.*

however, the *Trieste* just sat there because it did not have the technological capability to explore. Nevertheless, this

Crewmen tie up the U.S. Navy's deep submergence vessel Turtle *in San Diego Bay. While not exactly submarines, deep diving vessels operate much like submarines. They allow researchers to learn much about underwater life.*

is the deepest dive in history and the only attempt ever made to achieve so deep a dive.

Most of the submersible research vessels built since the *Trieste* have resembled a cross between diving spheres and submarines. While not submarines in the strictest sense, these vessels operate in much the same way as submarines, since submarine technology played a part in their development. In place of disposable ballast, the submersibles use water-ballast tanks that can be emptied by pressure from compressed air. Instead of merely diving and surfacing, they move around using one or more propellers. And rather than restricting scientists to the role of observers, these craft have mechanical manipulator arms and other tools that let scientists take samples of rocks, plants, and animals from the deep ocean.

In the last few years researchers in the United States and Japan have been building vessels that will let them study the ocean at greater depths and for longer periods than previously thought possible. One such modern research submarine, the Shinkai 6500 of Japan, has been hunting for bacteria that can be developed for commercial uses, such as dissolving oil spills. The sub, which can dive to more than four miles below the surface, already has brought back microorganisms from deep-ocean hot springs and other areas of the sea floor.

Other researchers are planning even deeper dives, including a return to the Challenger Deep. Initially, these dives will be made by remote-controlled robotic submersibles. A robotic vessel operated by the Japan Marine Science

The diving vessel Alvin *can take researchers to new depths for exploring the ocean floor. Some submersibles are equipped with tools that allow researchers to obtain samples of organisms found in deep water.*

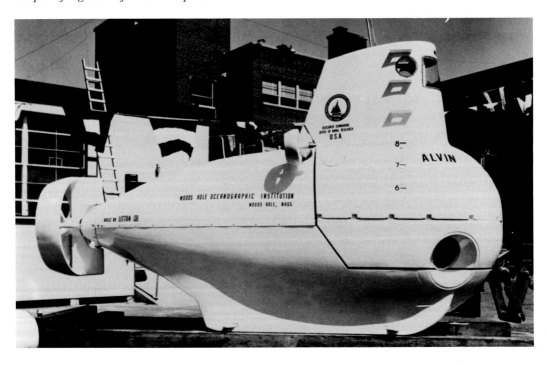

The navy's unusual research submarine, called the NR-1, is nuclear powered but very slow moving. The nuclear reactor on NR-1 allows the submarine to stay submerged at deep depths for extended periods.

and Technology Center is planned to make the first of the dives in 1993. And a California-based engineer named Graham Hawkes hopes to dive to the bottom of the Challenger Deep in 1996 in a one-person sub he designed. The sub, named *Deep Flight II*, is shaped somewhat like an airplane. If Hawkes's plan succeeds, researchers will be able to essentially fly underwater as they explore the ocean depths.

Nuclear-Powered Dives

For the past two decades the U.S. Navy has been operating one of the world's more unusual research submarines, the NR-1 (*NR* stands for nuclear research). The unique thing about the NR-1 is its power plant. The thirty-foot-long, fifteen-foot-tall vessel was built to test the capabilities of an experimental nuclear reactor and to conduct deep-water research that larger submarines cannot do. Despite its reactor the sub cannot travel very fast, limiting the distance it can go on its own. At most it can travel at four knots, or around five miles an hour. In order to get to its dive sites, it has to be towed by a larger, support ship, the USS *Sunbird*.

Despite its small size the NR-1 is a versatile machine. It can dive to roughly twenty-six hundred feet, or nearly half a mile, below the surface. Because of its nuclear power plant, it can stay under-water for twenty days at a time. For the crew, though, this means twenty days of cramped living conditions. The NR-1's engine room, including the small nu-clear reactor, takes up roughly two-thirds of the pressure hull. The remain-ing space houses the control station, a series of viewports that require re-searchers to lie on their stomachs, and bunks for only half the crew at one time.

The submarine is just as unusual on the outside. For one thing, the NR-1's designers took a page from Simon Lake's book and installed four wheels on the bottom of the hull. Just as Lake envisioned, the wheels allow the subma-rine to crawl along the sea floor. There are no air locks for divers, but re-searchers can record their findings from external television cameras and take samples with a remote-controlled mechanical arm.

In addition to its abilities as a re-search vessel, the NR-1 also has per-formed as a salvage ship for the navy. In 1976 the small submarine was called in to recover a Phoenix air-to-air missile that had fallen from an aircraft carrier off the coast of Scotland. Ten years later the sub was used to bring up wreckage of the space shuttle *Challenger*, which ex-ploded during its launch in January 1986.

Fulfilling Two Dreams

The submarine has changed forever the way people look at the oceans of the

Although the use of submarines as weapons of war may continue to decline, submarines show increasing potential as vessels of research and recreation.

Submarines may allow unparalleled access to unexplored waters, helping humans gain a greater understanding of the ocean depths.

world. Simply by voyaging beneath the waves submarines have helped to expand awareness about the marvels and hazards of the underwater world. Though their presence in naval operations worldwide may be reduced in the coming decades, submarines offer hope for new avenues of research and recreations. Perhaps one day submarine excursions—both recreational and scientific—to the deepest ocean trenches will be as easy as a trip to the Grand Canyon.

Submarine technology has come far in a very short time and will, undoubtedly, continue to develop in the future. Submarines of the twentieth century fulfilled John Holland's dream of a silent and efficient weapon of war. Perhaps, then, submarines of the twenty-first century will fulfill Simon Lake's dreams of unlimited underwater exploration.

Glossary

aft: In the rear of a submarine or a ship.

air lock: A small chamber used to let divers enter or leave a submarine.

ballast: A weight or combination of weights used to force a submarine underwater.

ballast tanks: Water tanks in or around a submarine's hull used to hold or expel water for ballast.

boats: Traditional navy nickname for submarines.

boomer: Navy nickname for a submarine that carries short-range or intercontinental ballistic missiles.

bow: The front end of a submarine or a ship.

class: A particular series or design group of submarine or surface ship.

conning tower: A structure on top of a submarine's hull, from which submariners steer while on the surface.

conventional submarine: A diesel-electric or other nonnuclear submarine.

depth charge: Can-shaped antisubmarine bomb fired from a surface ship. Also called ash can.

diesel engine: An internal combustion engine that uses high pressure instead of a spark plug to detonate fuel.

diving planes: Rectangular metal planks, mounted horizontally, used to submerge or raise a submarine.

fore: In the front of a submarine or a ship.

keel: The central supporting piece of a submarine's hull bottom; it runs the length of the submarine.

mine: An anchored underwater bomb.

outer hull: The outer casing of a double-hulled submarine. Also acts as a cover for the submarine's ballast tanks.

periscope depth: The depth at which a submerged submarine's periscope can rise above the surface of the ocean.

pressure hull: The casing of a submarine that protects the crew and equipment from the sea; the inner hull of a double-hulled submarine.

propeller: A fan-bladed device, mounted on a turning shaft, which moves a ship or a submarine.

Q-ship: A merchant ship equipped with hidden weapons and commissioned for submarine hunting by the British Royal Navy.

rudder: A wooden or metal plank that guides a ship or a submarine.

sonar: Acronym for *sound navigation and ranging*; a device that uses reflected sonic, or sound, waves to detect ships or other features underwater.

stern: The rear end of a submarine or a ship.

storage battery: A battery used to store electricity in a diesel-electric submarine for underwater operations. Also used in nuclear submarines as an emergency power supply.

submariner: A submarine sailor.

submersible: Able to submerge. Also, a vessel able to make excursions underwater.

torpedo: A self-propelled, sausage-shaped underwater weapon used to destroy surface ships or submarines.

torpedo tube: A tube that uses blasts of compressed air to fire torpedoes, missiles, or mines.

U-boat: The English contraction of *Unterseeboot* (under-sea boat), the German word for submarine.

wolf pack: A group of submarines assembled to make coordinated attacks on surface ship convoys.

For Further Reading

Robert D. Ballard, "NR-1, The Navy's Inner-Space Shuttle," *National Geographic*, April 1985.

Douglas Botting, *The U-Boats*. Alexandria, VA: Time-Life Books, 1979.

Robert F. Burgess, *Ships Beneath the Sea: A History of Subs and Submersibles*. New York: McGraw-Hill, 1975.

A.A. Hoehling and Mary Hoehling, *The Last Voyage of the Lusitania*. New York: Popular Library, 1957.

Jonathan Rutland, *See Inside a Submarine*. New York: Warwick Press, 1988.

Richard F. Snow, "The 'Holland' Surfaces," *American Heritage*, April/May 1984.

Works Consulted

"Death on a Mimic Sub," *Time*, May 9, 1988.

Tony Emerson and Hideko Takayama, "Down to the Bottom," *Newsweek*, July 5, 1993.

Bill Gunston, *Submarines in Color.* New York: Arco Publishing, 1977.

Edwin P. Hoyt, *Submarines at War.* New York: Stein and Day, 1983.

Edwin P. Hoyt, *U-Boats: A Pictorial History.* New York: McGraw-Hill, 1987.

David Miller, *An Illustrated Guide to Modern Submarines.* New York: Arco Publishing, 1982.

John E. Moore and Richard Compton-Hall, *Submarine Warfare: Today and Tomorrow.* Bethesda, MD: Adler and Adler, 1986.

Steven Pearlstein, "The Seawolf Is Plying the Choppy Waters of Budget Cuts," *The Washington Post National Weekly Edition*, May 11-17, 1992.

"Secrets of the Deep," *Popular Mechanics*, September 1986.

Richard Sharpe, *Jane's Fighting Ships 1991-92.* Alexandria, VA: Jane's Information Group, 1991.

Richard Sharpe, *Jane's Fighting Ships 1992-93.* Alexandria, VA: Jane's Information Group, 1992.

F.W. Tortolano, "Tomorrow's Submarine," *Design News*, August 20, 1990.

Gary E. Weir, *Building American Submarines 1914-1940.* Washington, DC: Naval Historical Center, 1991.

Index

Albacore (USS)
  unique design of, 67
Alexander the Great
  submarine tale and, 12
American Revolution
  submarine built during, 15-17
Argonaut, 30, 35-36
Athenia
  sinking of, 56
Atlantis Submarines International, 76

Baker, George, 30
ballistic missiles
  effect on submarines, 67-68
  on submarines
    description of, 71
Bangladesh, 70
bathyscaphe, 79
Bauer, Wilhelm
  inventor of *Sea Diver*, 20-22
  second submarine built by, 22
Borgeois, Simeon, 23
Botting, Douglas (*U-Boats*), 41
Brun, Charles-Marie, 23
Burgess, Robert F., 25
Bushnell, David
  inventor of *Turtle*, 15-17

Challenger, 82
Challenger Deep
  exploration of, 79-80
Champion, Bert, 35
Charles I, 15
Churchill, Winston, 56
Civil War
  submarines used during, 21
Cold War

end of, 74
  submarines use in, 11
Conqueror (HMS), 72
cruise missiles, 71

da Vinci, Leonardo
  submarine ideas of, 12
depth charges
  development of, 46-47
De Son
  submarine design of, 15
Dewey, George, 33
Diesel, Rudolf, 39
diesel engine
  description of, 39
Dönitz, Karl, 53-54, 56
  sets up antisubmarine warfare school,
    54-55
Drebbel, Cornelius van, 10
  first submarine and, 12-14
  method for taking in fresh air, 15

Eagle, 17
Electric Boat Company
  builders of first nuclear submarine, 63

Falaba
  sinking of, 45
Falklands
  use of submarines in, 70, 72
Fenian Ram, 27-29
Fenian Society, 25-26
  financiers of Holland project, 27
fox fire, 17
France
  electric submarines invented in, 23
  invention of submarine *Surcouf*, 51

Fulton, 34
Fulton, Robert
  inventor of *Nautilus,* 19-20

Garrett, G., 23
George Washington (USS), 68
Germany
  evaded war restrictions on sub
    building, 52-53
  first use of submarines in warfare, 22
  perfection of U-boats, 40-42
  reliance on submarines for attack
    vessels, 46
  use of submarines
    during World War I, 11, 42-43
      restrictions following, 49
    during World War II, 55-56
Golf class, 68
Great Britain
  antisubmarine devices of, 47
  blockade of America's ports, 17
  ended submarine building, 74
  proposed ban on submarines, 49-50
  purchase of submarines from John
    Holland, 34
  use of submarines
    during World War I, 40, 42-43
    in the Falklands, 70, 72
Gulflight
  sinking of, 45

Hall, Blakely, 27
Halstead, Oliver
  inventor of *Intelligent Whale,* 24
Hangor, 70
Hitler, Adolf, 52-53, 56
Holland, John, 30, 83
  retirement of, 35

submarines built by, 24-25
  Fenian Ram, 27-29
  for other nations, 34
  Holland I, 26
    problems with, 27
  Octopus, 34
  Plunger, 30-34
Holland I, 26
  drawbacks to, 38
Holland Torpedo Boat Company, 34
Holland (USS), 34
Hunley, Horace L.
  submarine design of, 21
Hunley (CSS), 21

I-boats, 52
India
  use of submarines, 70
Intelligent Whale, 24

James I (King)
  financed first submarine, 13, 15
Japan
  defeat of, 59-60
  development of submarines, 51-52
    during World War II, 56
  development of submersibles, 80
Japan Marine Science and Technology
  Center, 80-81

Korean War
  submarines used during, 60
Krupp, Gustav, 52
  role in building submarines, 53

Lake, Simon, 29
  inventor of *Argonaut,* 30
  private financing of *Argonaut,* 35

submarines sold to other nations, 36-37
Lockwood, Charles, 59
Lome, Dupuy de, 23
Louisville (USS), 72
Lusitania
  sinking of, 45

Nautilus, 20
Nautilus (USS)
  first nuclear submarine, 63-64
  records broken by, 65
Nordenfelt, Theodore, 23
North Pole
  use of submarines to explore, 77-78
NR-1, 81
  features of, 82
  use of as salvage ship, 82
nuclear deterrence, 69
  submarines used to enforce, 70
nuclear power
  use of in submarines, 63
nuclear submarine
  development of first, 63-64
  how it works, 66
  success of, 65

Oak Ridge laboratory, 62-63
Octopus, 34
Operation Desert Storm, 72

Pakistan
  use of submarines, 70
Pearl Harbor
  attack on, 57-58
Persian Gulf War
  submarines used during, 72
periscopes

description of, 50
Piccard, Auguste
  inventor of *Trieste*, 78-79
Plunger
  features of, 31-32
  problems with, 27
Protector, 36

Q-ships, 47

Redoubtables, 51
research
  submarines use in, 73-74
Rickover, Hyman, 67
  role in development of nuclear
    submarine, 63
  role in revamping U.S. Navy, 61-62
  role in testing first nuclear submarine,
    64
Roosevelt, Theodore, 32
rules of engagement, 43-44
Russia
  submarines purchased from Simon
    Lake, 36-37
Russo-Japanese War
  use of submarines in, 34

Scapa Flow
  Germany's attack on, 56
Sea Devil, 22
Sea Diver
  iron-hulled submarine, 20, 22
Seal, 37
Seawolf class, 74
Seawolf (USS), 65, 75
Simon Lake X, 37
Skate (USS), 65
  use of to explore North Pole, 78

Skipjack (USS), 67
sonar
  description of, 58
Soviet Union
  collapse of, 70
  ended submarine building, 74
  first nation to put missiles on
    submarines, 68
  first nuclear submarine, 68-69
Spanish-Amerian War, 33
submarines
  drawbacks to as merchant vessels, 76-
    77
  early
    fatalities associated with, 39
  effect of ballistic missiles on, 67-68
  first, 10, 12-14
  future uses of, 73
  golden age of, 73
  how they dive and surface, 28
  limitations of, 72
  limited warfare use of, 70
  modern costs of, 75
  more built after World War I, 51
  negative atttitude toward, 11
  non-military uses, 11
  obstacles to successful design of, 38
  steering of, 33
  uses of
    as surveillance vehicles, 57
    in exploration, 77
    in recreation, 75-76
  weapons of, 71
submersibles, 78-79
  robotic, 80-81
  use of in research, 80
Surcouf, 51
Sverdrup, Harald

exploration of North Pole using
  submarine, 77-78

Tirpitz, Alfred von, 44
Tomahawk, 72
torpedo, 71
  developments in, 51
  invention of, 32
  U.S.
    drawbacks to, 59
Trieste, 78-79
Turtle, 15-17
  attack on HMS *Eagle*, 17-19
  use of against Britain, 18-19

U-boats
  development of, 40-41
  features of, 41
  sinking of American and British ships,
    45
  success of, 48
  violations of rules of engagement,
    44-45
United States
  anger over *Lusitania*, 45
  cutbacks following World War II, 61
  development of missile-carrying
    submarines, 68
  development of submarines, 52
  development of submersibles, 80
  torpedoes
    drawbacks to, 59
  unprepared for World War II
    submarine warfare, 56-57
U.S. Navy
  first submarines built by, 24
  new plans for after World War II, 61
  use of submarines in decline, 75

Unterseebooten, 40

Verne, Jules, 29

warships
  rules followed by, 43-44
Washington, George, 17
Washington armament conference, 49
water
  as ballast, 14
Whitehall torpedoes, 32
Wilhelm, Kaiser, 44-45
Wilkins, George Hubert

exploration of North Pole using
  submarine, 77-78
World War I
  number of submarines used during,
  11, 40-41
  submarine battles in, 42-43
World War II
  as successful, 60
  Germany's success, 55-56
  submarines used during, 49

Zédé, Gustave, 23

About the Author

Sean M. Grady has had a varied career both as a journalist and as a free-lance writer. While attending the University of Southern California, he worked for the entertainment section of the *Los Angeles Times* as a reporting intern, for *California Magazine* as a research intern, and for the City News Service of Los Angeles—a local news wire—as a general assignment reporter. Graduating with a bachelor of arts degree in print journalism in 1988, Grady specialized in business reporting, eventually serving as business editor of the *Olympian*, a Gannett newspaper in Olympia, Washington. He has written a number of books for Lucent Books, including *The Importance of Marie Curie, Illiteracy,* and *Plate Tectonics.* Grady lives in Sparks, Nevada.

Picture Credits

Cover photo by © Bob Peterson/FPG International

Atlantis Submarines, 76 (both), 83

Culver Pictures, 18, 29

Deutschland Erwacht/Simon Wiesenthal Center Archives, Los Angeles, CA, 54

General Dynamics Electric Boat Division, 73, 82

Historical Pictures/Stock Montage, 13, 20, 21

Library of Congress, 26, 31, 44 (bottom), 45 (both), 49, 56

National Archives, 25, 55, 57 (top), 59, 60, 64 (top)

North Wind Picture Archives, 12, 14, 19 (top)

Official U.S. Navy Photo, 19 (bottom), 22, 24, 30, 32, 34, 35, 36 (both), 38, 40, 41, 42, 43, 44 (top), 46, 47, 48, 51, 52, 53 (both), 57 (bottom), 61, 62, 64 (bottom), 65, 67, 68, 69, 70, 72, 74 (both), 77, 78, 79 (both), 80, 81